GCSE
Physical Education

Complete Revision and Practice

Contents

UNIVERSITY OF CHICHESTER

CR
796
PAR

Published by Coordination Group Publications Ltd

Editors:
Alice Shepperson

Contributors:
Emma Cannell, Dee Crawford, Charley Darbishire, Steve Ireland, Sharon Keeley, Simon Little,
Tim Major, Glenn Rogers, Andy Park, Ami Snelling, Katherine Stewart, Claire Thompson, Sharon Watson

Also featuring Alice Shepperson's bottom as itself.

Illustrations by Sandy Gardner (e-mail: illustrations@sandygardner.co.uk) and Bowser, Colorado USA
With thanks to Chris Cope, Glenn Rogers and Ryan Whelan for the proofreading.

AQA material is reproduced by permission of the Assessment and Qualifications Alliance.
Edexcel (London Qualifications Ltd) examination questions are reproduced by permission of London Qualifications Ltd.
OCR examination questions are reproduced by permission of OCR.

ISBN-10: 1 84146 386 8
ISBN-13: 978 1 84146 386 5

Website: www.cgpbooks.co.uk
Printed by Elanders Hindson Ltd, Newcastle upon Tyne.
Clipart source: CorelDRAW® and VECTOR

Bones

The <u>skeleton</u> gives the body its <u>shape</u> and has loads of <u>jobs</u> to do. It's made up of various kinds of <u>bones</u>, all meeting at <u>joints</u> — and different joints move in different ways. Clever stuff.

The **Skeleton** is Made Up of **Bones**

The skeleton of an adult human is made up of <u>206 bones</u>.

Some of the most <u>important</u> ones are shown on the diagram opposite.

I'm afraid you're going to have to <u>learn them all</u>. Sorry...

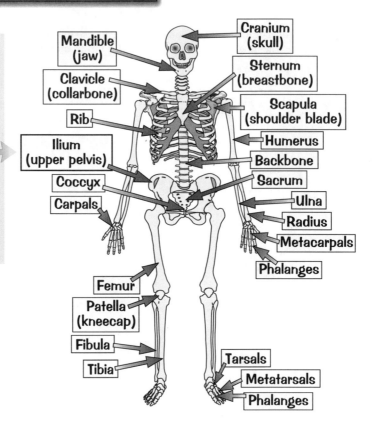

Cranium (skull)
Mandible (jaw)
Sternum (breastbone)
Clavicle (collarbone)
Scapula (shoulder blade)
Rib
Humerus
Ilium (upper pelvis)
Backbone
Coccyx
Sacrum
Carpals
Ulna
Radius
Metacarpals
Phalanges
Femur
Patella (kneecap)
Fibula
Tibia
Tarsals
Metatarsals
Phalanges

The **Skeleton** has Different **Functions**

① Support

1) The skeleton is a <u>rigid frame</u> for the rest of the body.
2) The skeleton <u>supports</u> the soft tissues.
3) Without the skeleton, we'd <u>collapse</u> like <u>jelly</u>.
4) For <u>example</u>, without ribs, our chests would collapse, preventing our lungs from working.

② Shape

1) Our <u>shape</u> is mainly due to our skeleton.

Exercise and **diet** are both important in maintaining **bone strength** throughout life.

③ Protection

1) Bones are very <u>tough</u>.
2) They <u>protect</u> delicate organs — like the <u>heart</u> and <u>lungs</u>.
3) For example, the skull protects the brain, like a crash helmet.

④ Movement

1) There are loads of <u>joints</u>.
2) <u>Muscles</u>, attached by tendons, can <u>move</u> various bones.

⑤ Making Blood Cells

1) <u>Long bones</u>, like the femur, contain <u>bone marrow</u>.
2) New <u>blood cells</u> are made in this bone marrow.

Bones — our closest supporters...

It may seem harsh, but you've got to learn the names of these bones. And their functions of course...

Bones

And that's not all. There's <u>loads more</u> to learn about bones...

Bones are formed by the Ossification of Cartilage

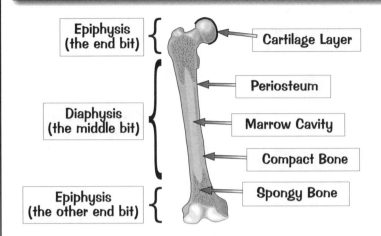

Epiphysis (the end bit) — Cartilage Layer

Diaphysis (the middle bit) — Periosteum, Marrow Cavity, Compact Bone

Epiphysis (the other end bit) — Spongy Bone

1) All bones start off as <u>cartilage</u> in the <u>womb</u>. They gradually turn to bone by <u>ossification</u> — but it takes <u>years</u> for some bones.

2) Bones have a <u>tough outer layer</u> called the <u>periosteum</u> — except where they've got cartilage instead.

3) <u>Spongy bone</u> is <u>light</u> but <u>tough</u>. Some spongy bone contains <u>red marrow</u>, where <u>red blood cells</u> are made.

4) The <u>marrow cavity</u> contains <u>yellow marrow</u>, where <u>white blood cells</u> form.

There are Four Different Types of Bone

Remember these different types of bone — you'll need to know them for the exam.

LONG BONES

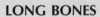

These include the <u>femur</u>, <u>humerus</u>, <u>tibia</u>, <u>radius</u>, etc... They're where blood cells are made.

SHORT BONES

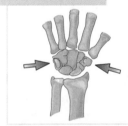

These include bones like the <u>carpals</u> (in the wrists) and the <u>tarsals</u> (in the ankles). They're designed to take a lot of weight and absorb the stresses of running and jumping.

FLAT BONES

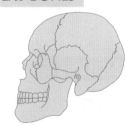

Some of the bones in the <u>skull</u> are flat.

IRREGULAR BONES

These are odd shaped bones like the <u>vertebrae</u> and the <u>pelvis</u>.

The Skeleton has a big effect on Performance

1) The skeleton has a huge effect on the <u>size</u> and <u>shape</u> of the body.

2) The skeleton determines a person's <u>height</u> and <u>optimum weight</u>.

3) The skeletal system is vital to <u>performance</u> — for example, people with <u>long</u>, <u>light</u> bones are likely to out-perform people with <u>short</u>, <u>dense</u> bones in sports like <u>basketball</u> or <u>high jump</u>.

4) <u>Bone strength</u> is also very important, especially in sports like rugby or weightlifting which put a lot of strain on the body.

Learn the bare bones — and then all the fiddly details as well...

And that's the skeleton. Are you sure you know exactly how bones work? If not, read it again.

Joints

Your <u>backbone</u> is <u>all-important</u>. And so is all that <u>connective tissue</u> — the string and glue that holds us together — maybe you'd better learn about that too...

The Spine has Five Different Sections

The <u>vertebral column</u> (or <u>spine</u>) is divided up into different sections, and each section contains some smallish bones called <u>vertebrae</u> (each one is a '<u>vertebra</u>').

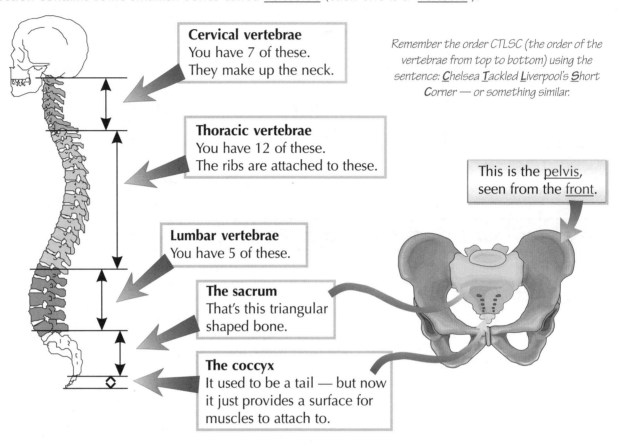

Cervical vertebrae
You have 7 of these.
They make up the neck.

*Remember the order CTLSC (the order of the vertebrae from top to bottom) using the sentence: **C**helsea **T**ackled **L**iverpool's **S**hort **C**orner — or something similar.*

Thoracic vertebrae
You have 12 of these.
The ribs are attached to these.

This is the <u>pelvis</u>, seen from the <u>front</u>.

Lumbar vertebrae
You have 5 of these.

The sacrum
That's this triangular shaped bone.

The coccyx
It used to be a tail — but now it just provides a surface for muscles to attach to.

Connective Tissues Join Muscle and Bones

There are <u>three types</u> of <u>connective tissue</u> you need to know about.

CARTILAGE	LIGAMENTS	TENDONS

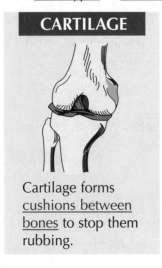

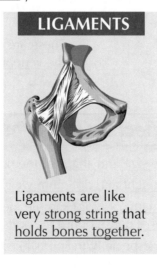

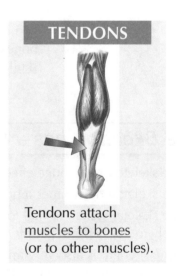

Cartilage forms <u>cushions between bones</u> to stop them rubbing.

Ligaments are like very <u>strong string</u> that <u>holds bones together</u>.

Tendons attach <u>muscles to bones</u> (or to other muscles).

Don't get ligaments and tendons confused...
Remember — ligaments connect bones with bones; tendons connect bones with muscles.

Joints

Yes, but how do joints actually <u>work</u>? Well, read and learn...

There are **Three** Different **Types** of **Joint**

<u>Not</u> all joints allow <u>movement</u>. There are <u>three</u> different types for you to know about:

Fixed, or **immovable** joints

These are also called <u>fibrous joints</u>.

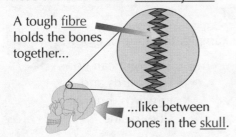

A tough <u>fibre</u> holds the bones together...

...like between bones in the <u>skull</u>.

Slightly movable joints

These are sometimes called <u>cartilagineous joints</u>.

Each of the bones rests on a cushion of <u>cartilage</u>...

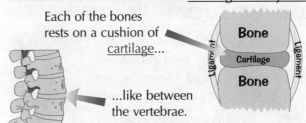

...like between the vertebrae.

The bones can move a <u>little bit</u> — but ligaments <u>stop</u> them moving too far...

Freely movable joints

These are sometimes called <u>synovial joints</u>.

These contain <u>synovial fluid</u> inside a pocket called the <u>synovial membrane</u>.
This <u>lubricates</u> (or 'oils') the joint.

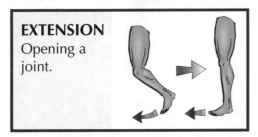

The <u>shoulder</u> joint is a freely movable joint.

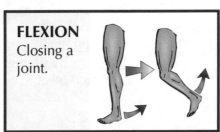

All the moving parts are held together by <u>ligaments</u>.

There are **Six Kinds** of Joint **Movement**

There are <u>six</u> different kinds of movement the joints can allow. You need to know them all.

EXTENSION
Opening a joint.

FLEXION
Closing a joint.

ADDUCTION
Moving towards an imaginary centre line.

ABDUCTION
Moving away from an imaginary centre line.

ROTATION
Turning a limb clockwise or anticlockwise.

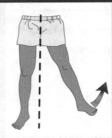

And <u>circumduction</u> is a <u>combination</u> of extension, flexion, adduction and abduction — so that a limb, finger, etc. traces out a <u>circle</u>. This is the movement you can do with your finger if your hand stays still.

No — Abduction has nothing to do with kidnapping...

Do you know the best way to make sure you've mastered a page like this? You cover up the page, get a piece of paper, and then scribble everything you've learnt down in as much detail as possible. Easy.

Joints

I bet you think you know the different types of joint — fixed, slightly movable and freely movable. Well, I'm afraid it's not quite that simple. There are different types of movable joint...

There are **Five Types** of **Movable Joint** you need to know

Your shoulder can move in more directions than your knee. That's because it's a different kind of joint. Here are the five kinds you'd better learn:

BALL AND SOCKET

For example, the <u>hip</u> or <u>shoulder</u>.

The joint can move in <u>all directions</u>, and it can <u>rotate</u> as well.

So this allows <u>flexion</u>, <u>extension</u>, <u>adduction</u>, <u>abduction</u> and <u>rotation</u>.

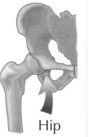

Hip

HINGE

For example, the <u>knee</u> or <u>elbow</u>.

The joint can go <u>backwards and forwards</u>, but not side-to-side.

This allows <u>flexion</u> and <u>extension</u>.

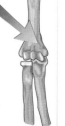

CONDYLOID

For example, the <u>wrist</u>.

The joint can move <u>forwards and backwards</u>, <u>left to right</u> — but it can't rotate.

Allows <u>flexion</u>, <u>extension</u>, <u>adduction</u> and <u>abduction</u>.

PIVOT

For example, the joint in your <u>spine</u> that lets you <u>shake</u> your head.

This joint is between the <u>atlas</u> and <u>axis</u> bones in your neck.

This kind of joint only allows <u>rotation</u>.

GLIDING

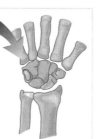

For example, between the <u>tarsals</u> or <u>carpals</u>.

The bones move a <u>little bit</u> in <u>all directions</u> by sliding over each other.

Your Muscles and Joints act as **Levers**

Joints <u>multiply</u> either the <u>force</u> of a muscle, or the <u>speed</u> of a movement.

When you bend your elbow, your biceps makes a <u>short</u> movement, but your hand makes a <u>larger</u> one — this means your hand moves more <u>quickly</u>.

Short, slow movement

Larger, quicker movement

Increase your speed and power — harness the power of the lever...

Yuck — even more little diagrams to look at and learn. Well, at least they make the page look pretty. Make sure you understand how each type of movable joint works, and the importance of levers.

Warm-Up and Worked Exam Questions

Warm-up Questions

1) How many bones are there in an adult human body — 26, 120 or 206?
2) What do bones protect — vital organs, muscles or joints?
3) What is the anatomical name for the thigh bone?
4) In joints, what is the name of the cushioning pad found between bones?
5) A hinged joint allows movement in two directions. One is flexion, what is the other?
6) Name the three types of connective tissue that join muscles and bones.

Worked Exam Questions

You will almost certainly get questions on bones — make sure you can follow these worked examples, then have a go at the questions on the next page.

1   What is the name of the process that turns cartilage to bone?

Ossification

(1 mark)

2   This question is about the role of the skeleton.

a) Making blood cells is one of the functions of the skeleton.
   Name three other functions of the skeleton.

Maintaining the body's shape.   You could also put
                                    "supporting soft tissues",
Allowing movement.   but you only need three
                                    functions to get the marks.
Protecting vital organs.

(3 marks)

b) Below are five kinds of movement that joints can allow. Complete the table below by identifying a different joint that allows each type of movement.

Type of movement	Example of Joint
Flexion	*knee*
Extension	*elbow*
Abduction	*hip*
Adduction	*shoulder*
Rotation	*neck/spine*

*There are other possible answers to this question.
For example, you could swap the positions of 'hip' and
'shoulder', because both allow abduction and adduction.*

(5 marks)

Exam Questions

1   Give the anatomical name for the bones labelled A-E below.

A ....

B ....

C ....

D ....

E ....

(5 marks)

2   Which part of a bone produces blood cells?

....

(1 mark)

3   There are three types of connective tissue that join muscles and bones.
Complete the table below to identify their functions.

Connective Tissue	Function
Cartilage	
Ligaments	
Tendons	

(3 marks)

4   a)   What type of joint is the shoulder joint?

....

(1 mark)

b)   Give another example of this type of joint.

....

(1 mark)

c)   What types of movement does a condyloid joint allow?

....

(2 marks)

Muscles

There's lots to know about the <u>muscular system</u>. Muscles are really important in sport (er... obviously), so you better learn this stuff well. Let's start with the basics...

Muscles are Made of Loads of Small *Fibres*

It's important you know what the <u>big important muscles</u> are called. Learn this diagram well.

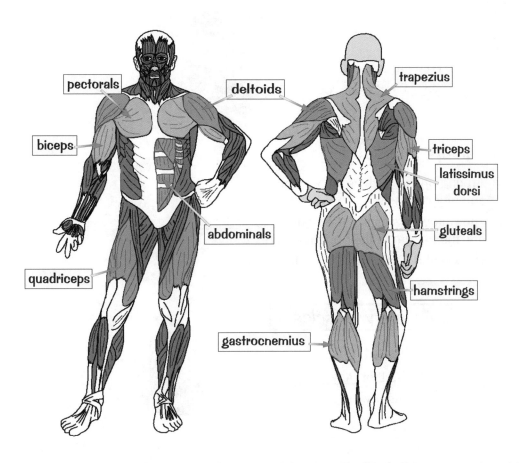

1) Muscles are made up of <u>fibres</u>.
   Only <u>some</u> of these fibres will be <u>ready to do work</u>.

2) All individual <u>voluntary muscle</u> fibres are either <u>fast-twitch</u> or <u>slow-twitch</u> (see the next page).

3) Everybody has a <u>similar number</u> of muscle fibres — but different people have <u>different proportions</u> of fast-twitch and slow-twitch fibres.

4) People who are <u>fit</u> and who have <u>larger muscles</u> have <u>fatter muscle fibres</u> — and more of their fibres are <u>ready</u> to be used.

5) <u>Nerve impulses</u> are what tell muscles to <u>contract</u> (or in the case of the heart, they tell it to speed up or slow down).

6) <u>Complex movements</u> are made possible by the <u>coordination</u> of nerve impulses sent to the muscles by the <u>nervous system</u>.

> Always use the **full names** of muscles. E.g. don't use 'quads' instead of 'quadriceps'.

AAARGHHH — Skinned people...

Right. There's only one thing for it. Draw some people (they don't have to look nice), and then label their muscles. You need to know these names, so get it done. Then get on with the next page.

9

Muscles

All muscles are not alike. Oh no, there are <u>different types</u>...

There are **Three** Different **Types of Muscle**

Like the title says, there are <u>three different types of muscle</u>. These are...

Cardiac Muscles

1) Only in the <u>heart</u>.
2) Contract and relax <u>continuously</u>.
3) Work <u>without conscious effort</u> from you.

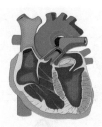

Involuntary Muscles

1) Around <u>organs</u> such as the <u>intestines</u>, and <u>blood vessels</u>.
2) They allow organs like the stomach to <u>stretch</u> and then <u>return</u> to their original size.
3) Work <u>without conscious effort</u> from you.

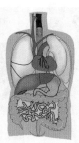

Voluntary Muscles

1) Attached to the <u>skeleton</u>.
2) Used for <u>movement</u>.
3) Under <u>your control</u>.

Fast-Twitch for **Power**, Slow-Twitch for **Endurance**

Fast-twitch fibres and slow-twitch fibres are good for <u>different things</u>.

<u>Fast-twitch fibres</u> contract very <u>quickly</u> and very <u>powerfully</u> — but they get <u>tired quickly</u>.

FAST RUNNER = FAST-TWITCH

Top-class <u>sprinters</u> and <u>shot-putters</u> have loads of <u>fast-twitch</u> fibres.

<u>Slow-twitch fibres</u> contract more <u>slowly</u> and with <u>less force</u> — but they <u>don't get tired</u> as quickly.

SLOW RUNNER = SLOW-TWITCH

Top-class <u>long-distance runners</u> have loads of <u>slow-twitch</u> fibres.

Learn the three muscle types — cardiac, voluntary and involuntary...

Ever wondered why some people are just slow at running, no matter how fit they are?
Well, a lack of fast-twitch muscle fibre probably has something to do with it...

SECTION ONE — THE HUMAN BODY

Muscles

You need to know about how muscles work in <u>pairs</u>, and all the fancy names that are used to describe this. All the info's here.

Muscles **Pull** on Bones

Muscles are attached to <u>two different bones</u> by <u>tendons</u>.

Only <u>one</u> of these bones will <u>move</u> when the muscle contracts.

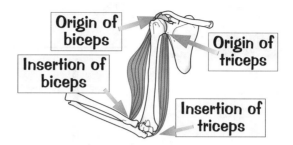

THE ORIGIN — The place where the muscle's attached to the stationary bone.

THE INSERTION — The place where the muscle's attached to the moving bone.

Antagonistic Muscles work in **Pairs**

Muscles can only do one thing — <u>pull</u>. To make a joint move in <u>two directions</u>, you need <u>two muscles</u> that can pull in <u>opposite directions</u>.

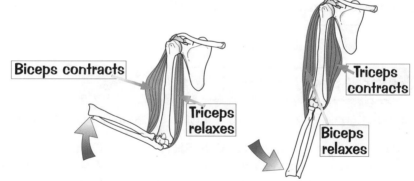

① <u>Antagonistic</u> muscles are <u>pairs of muscles</u> that work <u>against</u> each other.

② One muscle <u>contracts</u> (shortens) while the other one <u>relaxes</u> (lengthens) and <u>vice versa</u>.

③ The muscle that's doing the work (contracting) is the <u>prime mover</u> or <u>agonist</u>.

④ The muscle that's relaxing is the <u>antagonist</u>.

Synergists hold bones still

There are also muscles called **synergists**. They hold the stationary bone **still**, so only one bone moves — e.g. when the bicep contracts to bend the elbow, **synergists** stop the shoulder moving.

Antagonists — don't let them get to you...

Lots more horrid words to learn here, I'm afraid. I know — they're simply beastly! Still, they'll come in handy in the exam. Read the page again, cover it up, and then write down definitions of all the important terms — origin, insertion, antagonist, agonist, prime mover and synergist. Easy.

Muscles

You should also learn the effects of exercise and inactivity.

There are **Two** Types of **Muscle Contraction**

Muscles can perform two types of contraction — isometric and isotonic.

ISOMETRIC CONTRACTION

In an isometric contraction, the muscle stays the same length and so nothing moves.

Like if you pull on a rope attached to a wall.

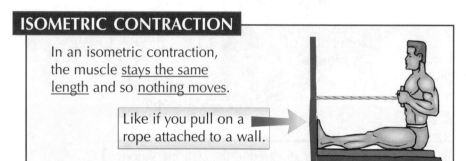

ISOTONIC CONTRACTION

In an isotonic contraction, the muscle changes length and so something moves.

Like if you exercise with weights that are free to move.

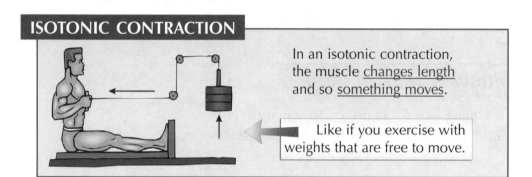

Effects of **Using Muscles** and **Muscle Tone**

If you use your muscles constantly, or underuse them, several things can happen.

MUSCLE FATIGUE
If you use your muscles a lot and they don't get enough oxygen, they feel tired or fatigued.

MUSCLE ATROPHY
If you don't use your muscles, they get smaller. This is atrophy.

CRAMP
A sudden contraction of a muscle that won't relax. Caused by a lack of salt minerals in the blood, or a lack of blood to a muscle.

Exercise improves **Muscle Tone**

Muscles never relax completely — there's always some tension in them. This is called muscle tone. Exercise improves muscle tone, which in turn improves your posture. If you improve your posture, you put less strain on your muscles, joints and bones, and you won't get injured as easily.

Exercise also causes muscles to get bigger.
The fibres become thicker and stronger, and the blood supply improves.
More of the muscle fibres are ready for immediate use.

Know your isotonic from your isometric...

I'm sure you already knew that exercise is good for your muscles, but you need to learn the details about why it's good. And don't forget to learn the effects of not exercising too. Don't get too hung up about isometric and isotonic — they're long words for very simple ideas. The diagrams should really help.

Warm-Up and Worked Exam Questions

Warm-up Questions

1) Muscles can only work in one direction — do they pull or push?
2) What is the name given to a pair of muscles that work against each other?
3) Are fast-twitch muscles better for speed or endurance?
4) Name the three different types of muscle
5) Muscles can contract in two different ways — isometric and isotonic.
   Which type of contraction causes movement?

Worked Exam Questions

Look through the worked examples and then have a go at the exam-style questions on page 13.

1   Muscles can be classified as voluntary, involuntary or cardiac.

   a)   Which type of muscle is found in each of these places?

        Attached to the skeleton *Voluntary muscles* ....

        In the heart *Cardiac muscle* ....

        In organs *Involuntary muscles* ....

                                                                                          (3 marks)

   b)   Explain how voluntary muscles differ from involuntary and cardiac muscles in
        how they function.

        Voluntary muscles are under our conscious control ....

        whereas involuntary and cardiac muscles are not. ....

                                                                                          (1 mark)

2   An athlete's suitability for a certain sport depends partly on the proportion of
     fast-twitch and slow-twitch muscle fibres they possess.

   a)   Explain why an athlete with a high proportion of fast-twitch muscle fibres would
        be better suited to sprinting than marathon running.

        Fast-twitch muscles contract very quickly/good for speed. ....

        Fast-twitch fibres contract very powerfully/produce a lot of force.

        Fast-twitch fibres tire quickly, so they're no good for endurance.
        There are three marks available here, so you need to make three separate points. *(3 marks)*

   b)   What is the function of a "synergist"?
        Synergist muscles hold some bones still while other muscles ....

        move nearby bones. ....

                                                                                          (2 marks)

Exam Questions

1   a)   Name the muscles labelled A-F on the diagram below.

A ....

B ....

C ....

D ....

E ....

F ....

(6 marks)

   b)   Muscles are attached to bones by tendons.
Explain what is meant by the terms "origin" and "insertion".

....

....

(2 marks)

2   Muscles work in antagonistic pairs to produce movement. Identify the agonist (prime mover) and the antagonist muscles used in flexing the leg at the knee joint.

....

....

(3 marks)

3   Complete the table below to define each term and identify its cause.

Condition	Definition	Cause
Muscle fatigue		
Muscle atrophy		
Cramp		

(3 marks)

The Respiratory System

The <u>respiratory system</u> includes everything we use to <u>breathe</u> and supply our bodies with <u>oxygen</u>. We breathe air into our <u>lungs</u>. The oxygen is then transferred to our <u>blood</u> and taken around our body.

The **Air** You Breathe **Ends Up** in the **Alveoli**

You'll need to know where the air goes on its way to the <u>alveoli</u>.

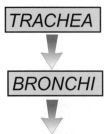

1) Air passes through the nose or mouth and then on to the <u>trachea</u>.

2) The trachea splits into two tubes called <u>bronchi</u> (each one is a '<u>bronchus</u>') — one going to each lung.

3) The bronchi split into progressively smaller tubes called <u>bronchioles</u>.

4) The bronchioles finally end at small bags called <u>alveoli</u> (each one is an '<u>alveolus</u>') where the <u>gas exchange</u> takes place.

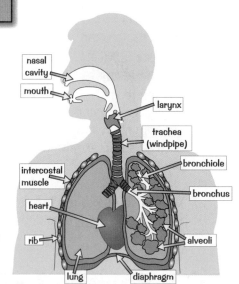

The area inside the chest containing the lungs, heart and all the other bits is the <u>chest cavity</u>.

Oxygen and **Carbon Dioxide** are **Exchanged** in the **Alveoli**

There are millions of alveoli in your lungs. This is where the <u>gaseous exchange</u> happens.

When you breathe:

1) <u>Carbon dioxide</u> moves from your blood into the <u>alveoli</u>.

2) <u>Oxygen</u> moves across to the <u>red blood cells</u>. The red blood cells contain <u>haemoglobin</u>, which combines with the oxygen to make <u>oxyhaemoglobin</u>.

3) The red blood cells <u>carry</u> the oxygen around the body and <u>deliver</u> it where it's needed. At the same time, the blood <u>collects carbon dioxide</u> to be taken back to the lungs.

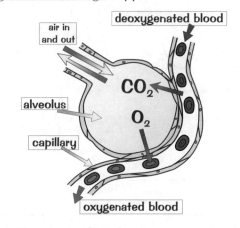

The air you breathe in and the air you breathe out are <u>different</u>. The air you breathe out has <u>less oxygen</u>, because the body's used some — but <u>more carbon dioxide</u>.

	You breathe in...	You breathe out...
Oxygen	21%	17%
Carbon dioxide	Only a tiny wee bit	4%
Water vapour	Not much	Quite a lot
Nitrogen + other inert gases	79%	79%

There is still <u>some oxygen</u> in the air you breathe out — that's why <u>mouth-to-mouth resuscitation</u> works.

The Respiratory System — oxygen in, carbon dioxide out...

Some pretty full-on Biology here, but it's not that complicated really. Like most things in Biology, this page is mainly about learning all the long words and what they mean. Spend a bit of time studying the diagrams — they should help the stuff on the rest of the page fall into place...

The Respiratory System

You'll need to know about <u>how you breathe</u> — and about the ways you can <u>measure</u> the <u>capacity</u> of your lungs. You also need to know how <u>exercise</u> affects your respiratory system.

The **Intercostal Muscles** and **Diaphragm** Make us Breathe

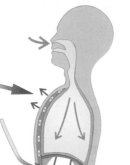

BREATHING IN (INSPIRATION):

1) The intercostals and the diaphragm <u>contract</u> and the <u>ribs move</u> upwards and outwards to make the chest cavity <u>larger</u>.

2) Air is pushed <u>into</u> the lungs by the <u>air pressure</u> outside.

BREATHING OUT (EXPIRATION):

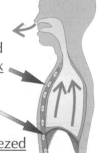

1) The intercostals and the diaphragm <u>relax</u> to make the chest cavity <u>smaller</u>.

2) The lungs are <u>squeezed</u> and air is forced <u>out</u>.

There are **Different Types** of **Lung Capacity**

A spirometer measures air breathed in and out, and produces graphs like this. From the graphs you can measure different lung capacities — which can be useful guides to health.

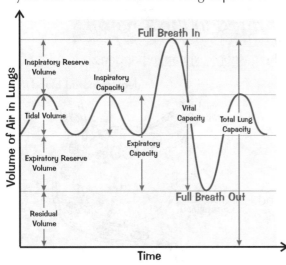

1 **TIDAL VOLUME** is the amount you breathe in (or out) with each breath.

2 **INSPIRATORY CAPACITY** is the most you can breathe in, after breathing out normally.

3 **EXPIRATORY RESERVE VOLUME** is the most air you could force out after breathing out normally.

4 **VITAL CAPACITY** is the most air you could possibly breathe in or out in one breath.

5 **RESIDUAL VOLUME** is the amount of air left in your lungs after you've breathed out as much as possible.

Exercise Increases Your **Oxygen Uptake**

When you <u>exercise</u>, your body needs <u>more oxygen</u> to make the muscles work. To achieve this:

1) You <u>breathe</u> more <u>quickly</u>,

2) Your <u>heart</u> pumps <u>faster</u> — so the red blood cells travel faster and <u>deliver more oxygen</u>.

That means your <u>oxygen uptake</u> increases. It's measured by your <u>VO_2</u>, which is just the <u>volume of oxygen</u> (O_2) your body uses in a <u>minute</u>. The maximum it reaches is called your <u>VO_2 Max</u> — the fitter you are, the higher it is.

How many ways can you measure lung capacity? — too many (sigh)...
The way to learn those breathing diagrams is to think about them. Feel yourself breathe in and out and try to relate it to the diagrams. It's the same with the lung capacities — they look hard at first, but give those complicated names a bit of thought and they'll soon make perfect sense...

Warm-Up and Worked Exam Questions

1) What gas does the body need in order to function — carbon dioxide, oxygen or methane?
2) Which blood cells carry oxygen around the body — red or white?
3) What do the chemical symbols O_2 and CO_2 represent?
4) What does your VO_2 max measure?
5) Where does gaseous exchange take place?
6) What effect does exercise have on your breathing rate?

Worked Exam Questions

Read through the worked examples and all the comments and tips that go with them. Once you've done that, you should be ready to have a go at the questions on the next page.

1   Describe the mechanisms involved in inspiration (breathing in). Mention all the structures that the air passes through.

The diaphragm and intercostal muscles contract, making the chest cavity larger, and drawing air in. Air passes into the mouth, down the trachea, through a bronchus, into the bronchioles and finally to the alveoli.

This question is asking for two things — the mechanisms of breathing in, and the structures through which the air passes. Make sure you cover both.

You don't need to talk about gas exchange — it's not part of inspiration.

(5 marks)

2   a)   Complete the table below to show the percentages of carbon dioxide and oxygen in the air we breathe in and the air we breathe out.

	Inhaled air	Exhaled air
Carbon dioxide	trace	*4%*
Oxygen	*21%*	17%

For questions like this, you'll usually get the mark if your answer is within 1% of the official answer.

(2 marks)

b)   Explain what happens in the lungs to produce this difference in composition between inhaled and exhaled air.

Gas exchange occurs at the alveoli — oxygen from the air moves into the blood. Carbon dioxide moves from the blood into the alveoli.

(2 marks)

Exam Questions

1   a)   Identify the parts of the respiratory system labelled A-E in the diagram below.

A ....

B ....

C ....

D ....

E ....

(5 marks)

b)   Briefly describe the gaseous exchange that takes place in the alveoli.

....

....

(2 marks)

2   The following phrases describe the mechanics of inhalation and exhalation.
Place a number in each of the spaces to put the phrases in the correct order, beginning
with inhalation. The phrase that comes first should be numbered '1'.

....   air is forced out of the lungs

....   the intercostal muscles and the diaphragm contract

....   a pressure difference draws air into the lungs

....   the intercostal muscles and diaphragm relax

....   the chest cavity becomes larger

....   the chest cavity becomes smaller.

(4 marks)

3   Lung capacity can be measured in different ways.

a)   Explain what is meant by the following terms:

Tidal volume ....

Vital capacity ....
(2 marks)

b)   Explain the immediate effects of exercise on oxygen uptake.

....

....

(2 marks)

The Circulatory System

Your circulatory system's pretty great. It comes in <u>two bits</u> — the pulmonary and systemic circuits.
The blood goes round one, then the other, passing through each side of the heart in turn.

The Circulatory System has **Three Functions**

TRANSPORT — moving things around the body in the
bloodstream, like oxygen, nutrients (like glucose), water and waste.

BODY TEMPERATURE CONTROL — more blood near the skin
cools the body quicker. That's why your skin looks redder after exercise.

PROTECTION — moving antibodies around the
body to fight disease. Blood clotting seals cuts.

The Human Heart is a **Double Pump**

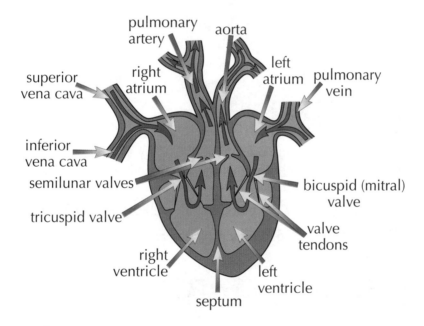

<u>Oxygenated</u> blood has <u>more oxygen</u>.
It's found in all <u>arteries</u> (except the pulmonary artery).

<u>Deoxygenated</u> blood has <u>less oxygen</u>.
It's found in all <u>veins</u> (except the pulmonary vein).

The <u>stroke volume</u> is the amount of blood pumped per beat.
You can use it to work out the amount pumped per minute:

The <u>heart rate</u> is the number of times the heart beats in one minute.

CARDIAC OUTPUT = STROKE VOLUME × HEART RATE

A good hearty page of facts — learn them all...

Another page, another diagram — and yes, you do need to learn all those piddling little labels. The
best way is to cover the page, make a rough sketch of the heart and then add all the labels you can
remember. There are fourteen labels in total. Make sure you go back and memorise any that you miss.

The Circulatory System

Humans have a Double Circulation

Each time a blood cell goes right round your body, it goes <u>through the heart twice</u> — that's <u>double circulation</u>. It happens because there are <u>two circuits</u>:

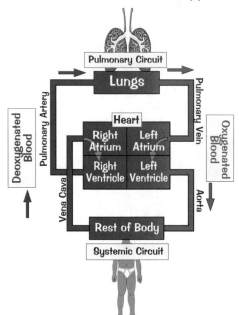

The **systemic circuit** is the main circuit. It carries:

1) <u>oxygenated blood</u> around the body in the <u>arteries</u>.

2) <u>deoxygenated blood</u> back to the heart along the <u>veins</u> — this then gets reoxygenated in the pulmonary circuit.

The **pulmonary circuit** includes the heart and lungs. It carries:

1) <u>deoxygenated blood</u> from the heart to the lungs to be oxygenated. The <u>oxygenated blood</u> then goes <u>back to the heart</u> to be pumped around the systemic circuit.

The Blood is Under Pressure

Your pulse is just the increase and decrease in pressure in the artery as your heart pumps blood. Blood pressure can be measured using a <u>sphygmomanometer</u>. It gives two readings:

SYSTOLIC PRESSURE — the pressure of the blood in the arteries when the <u>left ventricle contracts</u>.

DIASTOLIC PRESSURE — the pressure of the blood in the arteries when the <u>left ventricle relaxes</u>.

Blood Pressure is Affected by Loads of Things

These things affect your blood pressure:

AGE — blood pressure tends to increase with age.

GENDER — generally higher in men.

EXERCISE — increases blood pressure in the short term, but reduces it in the long term.

STRESS — increases blood pressure.

If your blood pressure remains high, you're at higher risk of these:

ANGINA — sharp pains in the chest, caused by the heart not getting enough oxygen.

HEART ATTACKS — the heart stopping because of oxygen starvation.

STROKES — damage to the brain because of oxygen starvation.

Avoid heart attacks and strokes — learn this page BEFORE the exam...

Make sure you can draw that circulation diagram and label it — you really do need to know the order in which blood flows though the heart, and where the oxygenated and deoxygenated blood goes. And don't forget to learn blood pressure — that section has the best word in the book — <u>sphygmomanometer</u>!

The Circulatory System

Here's some more about blood — gruesome...

There are **Three Types** of **Blood Vessel**

ARTERIES
Carry <u>oxygenated</u> blood <u>away</u> from the heart (except the pulmonary artery). They have thick, <u>strong</u> and <u>elastic walls</u> to cope with the <u>pressure</u>. Small arteries are called <u>arterioles</u>.

VEINS
Carry <u>deoxygenated</u> blood <u>back</u> to the heart (except the pulmonary vein). Have <u>thinner walls</u> than arteries because the blood is at a <u>lower pressure</u>. Veins have <u>valves</u> to keep the blood going in the right direction. Small veins are called <u>venules</u>.

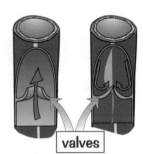

valves

CAPILLARIES
Carry <u>digested food</u> and <u>oxygen</u> directly to the tissues, and <u>take waste away</u> from them. Very <u>small</u> with very thin walls.

Blood is made up of **Cells, Platelets** and **Plasma**

RED BLOOD CELLS
Carry oxygen around the body in <u>haemoglobin</u>, the substance that gives blood its red colour.
They have <u>no nucleus</u>, leaving more space for haemoglobin.

WHITE BLOOD CELLS
Fight <u>against disease</u> by destroying:
1) <u>bacteria</u> using antibodies,
2) <u>toxins</u> using antitoxins,
3) foreign <u>microbes</u> by consuming them.

PLATELETS
Small <u>fragments</u> of cells with no nucleus. Platelets help the blood to <u>clot</u> at wounds.

PLASMA CARRIES EVERYTHING
in the bloodstream. That includes:
1) <u>Blood cells</u>,
2) Digested <u>food</u> (e.g. glucose),
3) <u>Waste</u> (e.g. urea, carbon dioxide),
4) <u>Hormones</u>.

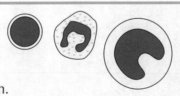

Blood, blood, glorious blood — nothing quite like it for...er...carrying oxygen...
Don't just skim the page — make sure you learn all the details about the different types of blood vessels and the different elements in the blood... Go on, it won't learn itself.

Warm-Up and Worked Exam Questions

Warm-up Questions

1) Which one of the following is not a function of the circulatory system — transporting oxygen, controlling body temperature or improving muscle size?
2) How many circuits are there in the circulatory system — one, two or five?
3) What type of blood is carried back to the heart (except in the pulmonary vein)?
4) Which type of blood vessel carries blood away from the heart?
5) Which type of blood cell carries oxygen?
6) Which type of blood cell fights disease?

Worked Exam Questions

Have a look at these, then move on to the next page for some real work...

1   List the three functions of the circulatory system.

Transportation (of oxygen/nutrients/water/waste),

control of body temperature,

protection/fighting disease

(3 marks)

2   a)   Name the parts labelled A to E in the diagram of a human heart below

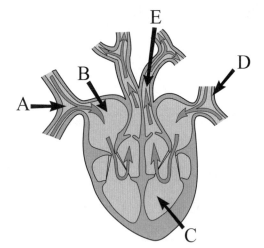

A   *vena cava*

B   *right atrium*

C   *left ventricle*

D   *pulmonary vein*

E   *aorta*

(5 marks)

b)   Describe the differences between the pulmonary circulation and the systemic circulation of blood.

Pulmonary — carries deoxygenated blood from the heart to the

lungs and oxygenated blood back to the heart. Systemic — carries

oxygenated blood around the rest of the body.

Say what type of blood is being moved, not just where it's going.   *(3 marks)*

Exam Questions

1   The diagram below is of a human heart.
    Identify the parts labelled A-D and describe what they do.

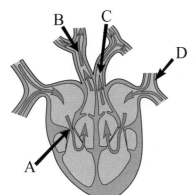

Part	Name	Function
A		
B		
C		
D		

(8 marks)

2   a)   Identify three factors that can affect blood pressure.

    ....

    ....

    ....
    (3 marks)

    b)   Complete the table below to identify the different types of blood vessels,
         their functions and the thickness of their walls.

Type of blood vessel	Function	Thickness of walls
	Carry oxygenated blood away from the heart	
Veins		
		Very thin

(6 marks)

3   Which components of the blood perform the following functions?

    a)   carry oxygen around the body   ....

    b)   fight against disease   ....

    c)   help the blood to clot   ....

    d)   carry everything in the bloodstream   ....
    (4 marks)

Revision Summary for Section One

Right, it's the end of the first section — well, almost. You could just call it a day and go on to the next section, but I wouldn't recommend it. Now's the perfect time to test what you've learnt and reinforce it in your brain. It really won't take that long either — and it's certainly a lot quicker than not doing it and then having to relearn it all later. Right, here's a load of questions then. Don't expect to be able to answer them all straight away, but do aim to be able to answer them all eventually.

1) Draw a rough sketch of the human skeleton and label as many bones as you can. You should be able to stick 23 labels on it.

2) Name five functions of the skeleton.

3) Bones are divided into four types depending on their shape. Name the four different types.

4) Draw a spine and label the different kinds of vertebra. How many are there of each?

5) What type of connective tissue joins bones to bones? And what's the point of cartilage?

6) Draw a picture of: a) a fixed joint, b) a slightly movable joint, and c) a freely movable joint. Don't forget to label all the various bits.

7) Name five types of movement at a joint. (Make sure you can give their proper names and also describe the movement they produce.)

8) Name five types of movable joint. Give an example of each type, and say what kinds of movement each type of movable joint will allow.

9) What do muscles and joints act as: a) levers, b) pulleys, or c) cranes?

10) Name the three different types of muscle, and give an example of each type. What are the differences between them?

11) What are the main muscles of the human body? Either label a sketch, or make sure you can name them on your own body. You should be able to name 11 muscles.

12) What are the differences between fast-twitch and slow-twitch muscle fibres? (And I don't mean just the obvious difference.) Name some sports that each type is suited to.

13) Are muscles attached to bones by: a) ligaments, b) tendons, c) cartilage, or d) string?

14) What's the fancy name for where a muscle attaches to a point on: a) a stationary bone, and b) a moving bone?

15) An antagonist relaxes while an agonist does work. TRUE or FALSE?

16) What does a synergist do?

17) What are isotonic and isometric contractions?

18) What is muscle atrophy? And what is cramp?

19) Draw a rough sketch of the chest cavity, and mark on all the bits of the respiratory system.

20) Where does gaseous exchange take place? What gases are exchanged?

21) How is the air you breathe in and the air you breathe out different?

22) What are the technical terms for breathing in and breathing out?

23) Draw a diagram to show how you breathe in, and another one to show how you breathe out.

24) Explain these terms: a) tidal volume, b) vital capacity, c) residual volume.

25) What does your VO_2 measure? What does VO_2 max mean?

26) Name three functions of the circulatory system.

27) Draw a diagram showing the heart and the two circuits that the blood travels round.

28) What are the two readings given when blood pressure is measured? Why are they different?

29) Name four things that affect blood pressure, and three things you're at risk of if your blood pressure is high.

30) Name the three main types of blood vessel.

31) Name the two main types of blood cell. What does each of them do? What's the liquid called that makes up the rest of the blood?

Health

Everyone wants to be healthy. You should be able to say what health actually is, and some of the things that can affect it — either for better or worse. Here we go...

Health is a State of **Well-being**

Remember this definition of health — it's the one used by the World Health Organisation (WHO).

> "Health is a state of complete physical, mental and social well-being, and not merely the absence of disease or infirmity."

PHYSICAL WELL-BEING:

1) Your heart, kidneys, and the rest of your body are working well.
2) You're not suffering from any diseases.
3) You don't have any injuries.

MENTAL WELL-BEING:

1) You don't have too much stress or anxiety.
2) You're not suffering from any mental illnesses.
3) You feel content.

SOCIAL WELL-BEING:

1) You have food, clothing and shelter.
2) You have friends.
3) You believe you have some worth in society.

For **Health**, Remember **PLEASED**

There are quite a few things that can affect your health. You need to know what they are, and the effects each one has. If you learn PLEASED, you won't go far wrong. Simple really.

P → **PERSONAL HYGIENE:** Keep yourself clean — it'll help you to avoid loads of diseases. It won't do your social life any harm, either.

L → **LIFESTYLE:** This is everything you do — including your job and your hobbies. A healthy lifestyle will include some physical exercise and some time to relax.

E → **EMOTIONAL HEALTH:** Feeling good is important. Try to avoid too much stress and worry. This can be caused by friends and relationships as well as things like work.

A → **ALCOHOL / DRUG USE:** Misuse of substances can lead to poor health. That includes alcohol and tobacco. Even breathing in other people's smoke (passive smoking) can lead to poor health.

S → **SAFETY:** If you have a dangerous job or hobby, you're more likely to injure yourself. So use the proper safety equipment — and in sport, play by the rules.

E → **ENVIRONMENT:** Pollution can cause respiratory problems. Noise can cause stress and affect your sleep.

D → **DIET:** You need the right balance of nutrients so you can cope with your lifestyle.

Learn this stuff — it's good for you...

There's a lot more to health than just not being ill — and that's something you'll need to be aware of in the exam. The things that can affect health are easy to learn if you just remember the PLEASED rule...

Fitness

There are two different kinds of fitness — and you need to know about both of them. It's also important to know what factors can affect fitness.

Fitness can be General or Specific

There are two basic kinds of fitness — general fitness, and specific fitness.

GENERAL FITNESS

This means you're able to meet the demands of your environment — you can do everyday activities without feeling too tired. For this, you need the four S's.

1) Strength	3) Stamina
2) Speed	4) Suppleness

General fitness also includes:

1) Cardiovascular endurance (aerobic fitness) — so your muscles can get enough oxygen to work properly.
2) Muscular endurance — so your muscles don't get tired too quickly.
3) Good body composition — you shouldn't be too fat or too thin.

SPECIFIC FITNESS

This is fitness to play a sport at a high level — and it needs good general fitness, as well as some or all of these...

1) Agility — to change direction quickly.
2) Balance — so you don't fall over.
3) Coordination — to move accurately and smoothly.
4) Explosive strength — brute strength combined with speed.
5) Fast reactions — to respond quickly.
6) Good timing — so you can act at just the right moment.

These are almost the first seven letters of the alphabet — ABC-EFG. Only 'D' is missing.

Fitness is Affected by HIP DAD

You can control some factors affecting fitness, but not others. Learn these HIP DAD factors.

H ➤ HEIGHT, WEIGHT & SOMATOTYPE* — Your basic shape can affect how good you can become at certain activities.

I ➤ ILLNESS & INJURY — They can affect fitness, either temporarily or permanently.

P ➤ PSYCHOLOGICAL FACTORS — The stress and tension of preparing for a big competition are examples of these.

D ➤ DISABILITIES — They can affect fitness. But by concentrating on particular activities, you can still reach a high level of fitness.

A ➤ ALCOHOL, DRUGS & SMOKING — They all have a negative effect on health and general fitness, in both the short and long term.

D ➤ DIET — This needs to contain the right balance of the different types of nutrient.

See page 45 for more about somatotypes.

Cardiovascular Fitness and Muscular Fitness

Cardiovascular (CV) fitness and muscular fitness are things you need to know about for the exam.

CARDIOVASCULAR FITNESS

This is about keeping your muscles supplied with oxygen. If your heart and lungs can provide a lot of oxygen, your CV fitness (or CV endurance) is good.

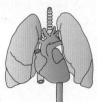

MUSCULAR FITNESS

This is good if your muscles can apply a lot of force to something. Basically, this means you can push, pull, lift, throw etc. very hard or very quickly.

Remember — there are 4 S's in fitnessss...

This page is full of memory aids: 'the 4 S's', 'ABC-EFG' and 'HIP DAD'. They do really help — so use them. Keep a separate note of all these aids, along with what they're helping you to remember.

Exercise

Exercise is physical activity done <u>primarily</u> to improve your health and fitness.
Learn what affects the <u>amount of exercise</u> different people need, as well why exercise is good for you.

Exercise Helps *Physically*, *Mentally* and *Socially*

There are <u>loads</u> of very good reasons for exercising. These reasons fall into <u>three basic groups</u>:

PHYSICAL BENEFITS

1) Improves your <u>body shape</u>, <u>muscle tone</u> and <u>posture</u>.
2) Strengthens the <u>bones</u>, reduces the chances of <u>illness</u> and increases <u>life expectancy</u>.
3) Increases your <u>strength</u>, <u>endurance</u>, <u>flexibility</u> and overall <u>fitness</u>.

MENTAL BENEFITS

1) Gives you a <u>challenge</u>, and a goal to aim for.
2) Helps you deal with <u>stress</u> and <u>tension</u>, and it can be <u>fun</u>.
3) Helps you to <u>feel better</u> about yourself and increase your <u>self-confidence</u>.

SOCIAL BENEFITS

1) Can improve your <u>teamwork</u> and <u>cooperation</u>.
2) Can help you <u>meet people</u> and lead to new friendships.
3) Sport can also improve your <u>image</u> and bring in <u>money</u>.

Different People Need *Different Amounts* of *Exercise*

Not everyone will need (or want) the same amount of exercise. It all depends on a person's...

PHYSICAL CONDITION
It's good to take things <u>easy</u> or see a <u>doctor</u> before starting to exercise if you've...

1) <u>Not exercised</u> for quite a long time,
2) Been <u>ill</u> for a while,
3) Reached <u>middle age</u>.

LONG-TERM GOALS
You'll need <u>different amounts</u> of exercise, depending on what your <u>goal</u> is...

1) To walk up stairs without feeling <u>out of breath</u>,
2) To do a <u>5-mile</u> fun run,
3) To win an <u>Olympic gold medal</u> for rowing.

Exercise Doesn't Have to be *Hell*

You can <u>hurt yourself</u> exercising if you're not careful. Here are some <u>guidelines</u> that should help...

1) Exercise should be <u>regular</u> — so establish a routine. Exercising <u>4 times</u> a week for 20 minutes will really help.
2) Start with gentle exercises and <u>increase the intensity</u> as you get fitter.
3) <u>Don't overdo it</u>. You shouldn't feel there's 'no gain without pain'. That's not true.

You can get good exercise by just changing a few <u>bad habits</u>...
1) <u>Walk</u> or <u>cycle</u> short distances, instead of taking a bus or going by car.
2) Don't take the lift — <u>use the stairs</u>.

Pain is weakness leaving the body... (at least that's what I tell myself after the first 10 miles).
Like with most things in life (except revising for your PE exam), exercise is best done in moderation.

Warm-Up and Worked Exam Questions

Warm-up Questions

1) Which one of these is not important for health — physical well-being, good reactions or mental well-being?
2) Name two widely used legal drugs that can badly affect health.
3) Explain the difference between general and specific fitness.
4) Explain the difference between cardiovascular and muscular fitness.
5) What are the four S's involved in general fitness?
6) Why do different people need different amounts of exercise?

Worked Exam Questions

Look at these worked examples. Make sure you note how much detail is included in each answer, and how this compares to the number of marks available. Then apply what you've learned.

1   "Health is a state of complete physical, mental and social well-being, and not merely the absence of disease or infirmity."

    a)   Explain the terms physical, mental and social well-being.

       Physical — body systems functioning well. No disease or injury.

       Mental — no mental illness, not stressed.

       Social — have food, shelter, friends and good self-esteem.

       (3 marks)

    b)   Explain how having a disability can affect your health.

       Disabilities can make exercise difficult, causing lack of fitness. However,

       good fitness can be achieved by doing activities suited to each individual.

       It's a two mark question, so you need to say more than just one simple statement.   *(2 marks)*

2   General fitness allows you to meet the demands of your environment.

    a)   What advice would you give to someone who hasn't exercised for a long time, but wants to improve their general fitness?

       Maybe see a doctor first. Start off very slowly and gradually increase

       intensity / duration. Establish a regular routine. Set goals.

       This answer goes into a bit more detail than is needed to get the marks, but if you know it, you might as well write it down.   *(2 marks)*

    b)   Competitive sports often require specific fitness. For any named sport, identify two specific fitness components necessary to perform well, and explain why they are important.

       Football requires speed to outrun an opponent to the ball and strength

       so as not to be pushed off the ball in tackle situations.

       Of course, there are many other possible answers. You'll get a mark for each component and a mark for explaining each one properly.

       (4 marks)

Exam Questions

1   Health and fitness are two different things.

    a)   Give two reasons why a person could be described as unhealthy, despite being physically fit.

       ....

       ....

       (2 marks)

    b)   Taking part in exercise produces physical, mental and social benefits.
       Give an example of each type of benefit for a sport of your choice.

       ....

       ....

       ....

       (3 marks)

2   Complete the table below to show the types of fitness required by different athletes.

Sport	Fitness component	Used for
Football		Turning quickly on the ball
Tennis	Coordination	
Basketball		To jump high for rebounds
Marathon		To keep going the whole distance
Sprinter	Fast reactions	

       (5 marks)

3   a)   Define the term "cardiovascular fitness".

       ....

       (1 mark)

    b)   Suggest one way of improving cardiovascular fitness.

       ....

       (1 mark)

    c)   Cardiovascular fitness is not the only type of fitness.
       What type of fitness would be most important to a weightlifter? Explain why.

       ....

       ....

       (2 marks)

The Effects of Exercise

When you start to exercise, your body has to make sure that your muscles get the <u>oxygen</u> they need so they can keep working. It also has to <u>avoid overheating</u>. It's all clever stuff.

*Your Body **Moves Up a Gear** When You Exercise*

To keep your muscles supplied with oxygen, these changes 'kick in' when you start to exercise.

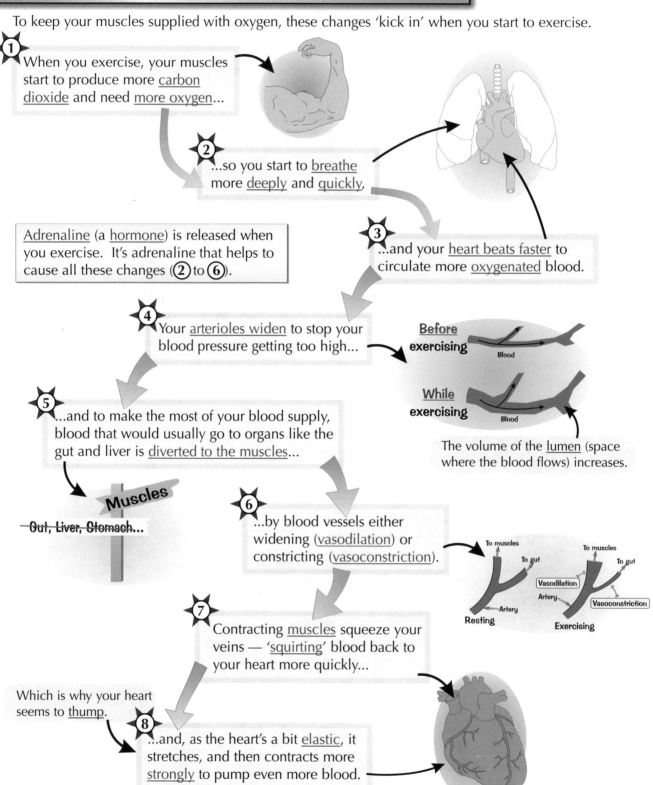

1 When you exercise, your muscles start to produce more <u>carbon dioxide</u> and need <u>more oxygen</u>...

2 ...so you start to <u>breathe</u> more <u>deeply</u> and <u>quickly</u>,

<u>Adrenaline</u> (a <u>hormone</u>) is released when you exercise. It's adrenaline that helps to cause all these changes (**2** to **6**).

3 ...and your <u>heart beats faster</u> to circulate more <u>oxygenated</u> blood.

4 Your <u>arterioles widen</u> to stop your blood pressure getting too high...

Before exercising
Blood

While exercising
Blood

The volume of the <u>lumen</u> (space where the blood flows) increases.

5 ...and to make the most of your blood supply, blood that would usually go to organs like the gut and liver is <u>diverted to the muscles</u>...

Muscles

~~Gut, Liver, Stomach...~~

6 ...by blood vessels either widening (<u>vasodilation</u>) or constricting (<u>vasoconstriction</u>).

To muscles
To gut
Artery
Resting

To muscles
To gut
Vasodilation
Artery
Vasoconstriction
Exercising

7 Contracting <u>muscles</u> squeeze your veins — 'squirting' blood back to your heart more quickly...

Which is why your heart seems to <u>thump</u>.

8 ...and, as the heart's a bit <u>elastic</u>, it stretches, and then contracts more <u>strongly</u> to pump even more blood.

More exercise means more oxygen is needed...

The point of all the changes that take place in your body when you exercise is to keep your muscles supplied with the extra oxygen they need. Make sure you learn all the changes, and in the right order.

The Effects of Exercise

Exercise doesn't just make your heart beat faster and your lungs work harder — it makes you <u>hotter</u> too...

Blood is **Shunted** to Control **Body Temperature**

1 As your muscles work, they <u>generate heat</u> — which warms your blood...

Which makes you go red.

2 ...and so this blood is <u>shunted</u> closer to your <u>skin</u>, so the heat can <u>escape</u> through radiation.

3 And you also start to <u>sweat</u>, which helps keep you cool.

'Shunting' blood means <u>diverting</u> it to where it's most <u>needed</u>.

Recovery Time Depends on Fitness

After all that, it takes a while to return to normal when you stop:

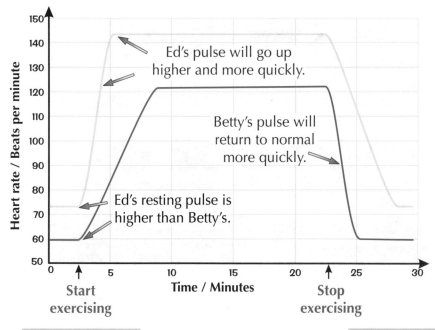

Ed's pulse will go up higher and more quickly.

Betty's pulse will return to normal more quickly.

Ed's resting pulse is higher than Betty's.

Heart rate / Beats per minute

Time / Minutes

Start exercising

Stop exercising

Betty's fit.

Ed's unfit.

RECOVERY TIME
This depends on
1) How <u>strenuous</u> the exercise was,
2) How <u>fit</u> you are.

LACTIC ACID REMOVAL
You still need <u>lots of oxygen</u> when you stop exercising to get rid of <u>lactic acid</u> — you must 'repay' the <u>oxygen debt</u>.

HEART RATE
When you stop exercising, your <u>heart rate falls</u> to its normal rate. The <u>fitter</u> you are, the <u>faster</u> it falls.

MUSCLE REPAIR
Muscles may get slightly <u>damaged</u> during exercise, and need to be <u>repaired</u>.

GLYCOGEN STORES
It takes up to <u>48 hours</u> to replace the <u>glycogen</u> used up.

It's surprising how long it can take to fully recover...

It's dead important that you learn about the 'shunt' of blood towards the skin and the muscles when you exercise. But then, recovery rates are pretty important too... oh, just learn it all.

The Effects of Exercise

Exercise makes your body change in more <u>permanent</u> ways too. The positive effects of regular exercise stay with you <u>long after</u> the end of the exercise session. All the stuff you need to know is here.

Aerobic Training Helps Your *Breathing* and *Circulation*

<u>Aerobic training</u>, where your heart and lungs work hard for a long time, does your <u>circulatory</u> and <u>respiratory</u> systems a power of <u>good</u>.

CIRCULATORY SYSTEM

1) Your body makes <u>more red blood cells</u> — so it can transport more oxygen.

2) Your <u>arteries get bigger</u> and '<u>stretchier</u>' — so your blood pressure falls.

3) More <u>capillaries</u> form in your <u>muscles</u>, so oxygen is delivered more efficiently.

4) Your <u>heart gets bigger</u> (just like when you exercise other muscles), and the walls of the heart get a bit <u>thicker</u>.

5) After exercising, your <u>heart rate</u> falls more <u>quickly</u> to its <u>resting level</u>.

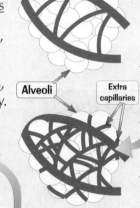

Alveoli

Extra capillaries

A bigger heart means a <u>bigger stroke volume</u>, and so your heart can beat more <u>slowly</u> and still pump the same amount of blood.

RESPIRATORY SYSTEM

1) The <u>diaphragm</u> and <u>intercostal muscles</u> get <u>stronger</u> — so they can make your chest cavity larger.

2) With a larger chest cavity, you can <u>breathe more air</u> in — so your <u>vital capacity</u> increases.

3) More <u>capillaries</u> grow around the <u>alveoli</u> — so more carbon dioxide and oxygen can be swapped at any time.

4) Because <u>gas exchange</u> is <u>quicker</u>, you can keep up vigorous exercise for longer.

Training is also *Good For You* in Loads of Other Ways

It's not just aerobic training that does you good — other kinds of exercise are also <u>beneficial</u>.

ENDURANCE TRAINING

1) Makes your body better at using <u>fat</u> for energy.

2) Makes your <u>muscles</u> more <u>efficient</u> at using <u>oxygen</u>.

3) Increases your VO_2 Max — the amount of oxygen your body can use in a minute.

4) Makes more <u>capillaries</u> form around your <u>muscles</u> and <u>alveoli</u>, so more oxygen can be supplied.

The process of making more capillaries is called <u>capillarisation</u>.

ANAEROBIC TRAINING

1) Makes the walls of the heart <u>thicker</u> (they're only muscle, after all).

2) Makes your muscles able to <u>put up</u> with <u>lactic acid</u> for longer — and they also get better at <u>getting rid</u> of it.

There's more about anaerobic activity on page 37.

STRENGTH TRAINING

1) Makes your muscles <u>thicker</u> so they can contract more <u>strongly</u> — this thickening is called <u>hypertrophy</u>.

2) Makes your <u>tendons bigger</u> and <u>stronger</u>.

And exercise helps your body in <u>yet more ways</u>. Read and learn this stuff, too.

JOINTS	BONES	BODY FAT
1) Exercise makes your <u>ligaments stronger</u>, and your <u>cartilage thicker</u>. 2) Regular <u>stretching</u> improves your <u>flexibility</u>.	Exercise makes your <u>bones stronger</u>.	When you train <u>regularly</u>, <u>fat</u> is burnt more <u>quickly</u> — whether you're exercising or resting — so you get <u>slimmer</u>.

Train that brain — start by learning this page...

If you remember ABC, you'll be able to remember this first section — Aerobic training helps Breathing and Circulation. As for the other stuff — just cover the page and see if you can write it all down...

Warm-Up and Worked Exam Questions

Warm-up Questions

1) What happens to your heart rate when you exercise?
2) What happens to your breathing when you exercise?
3) How does your fitness affect your recovery rate after exercise?
4) Describe what is meant by aerobic exercise.
5) What's meant by a short-term effect of exercise and a long-term effect?
6) How does strength training affect your muscles?

Worked Exam Questions

Here's another load of questions to have a go at. The first ones are done for you.

1   Exercise causes changes to the body.

a)   List three immediate effects of exercise on the human body.

Heart rate increases.

Breathing gets deeper and quicker.

Sweating occurs.

(3 marks)

b)   Identify two factors that affect recovery time after exercise.

Intensity of exercise.

The person's fitness

(2 marks)

The word 'regular' indicates that the question is about the long-term effects of exercise.

2   a)   Explain the effects of regular aerobic training on the circulatory system.

More red blood cells are produced. Arteries get bigger and blood pressure decreases. More capillaries form around muscles. The heart gets bigger and its walls thicken, so it pumps blood more efficiently.

(3 marks)

b)   Explain the effects of regular anaerobic training on the muscular system.

Bigger/stronger muscles (hypertrophy). Body becomes able to cope with higher levels of lactic acid for longer and gets more efficient at removing it. Stronger tendons/ligaments.

(3 marks)

Exam Questions

1   The diagram below shows the heart rates of two students, Dee and Paddy, during a
training session. Both students worked at the same intensity.

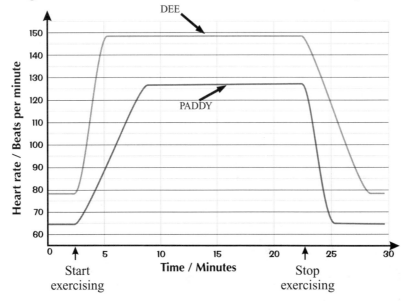

Which of the two students do you think is fitter?
Explain how you can tell this from the graph.

....

....

....

....

(4 marks)

2   Exercise affects the body in many ways, both immediately and in the long term.

a)   Identify three long-term effects of regular aerobic training on the respiratory
system.

....

....

....

(3 marks)

b)   Give two reasons why breathing and heart rate remain high for a while after
exercise has stopped.

....

....

(2 marks)

Diet and Nutrition

"You are what you eat," people sometimes say — that's how vital this subject is. It's very important to know about <u>different foods</u>, what they contain, and why we need to eat them.

You need a Balance of *Protein*, *Carbohydrate* and *Fat*

Protein, carbohydrate and fat make up the bulk of your food. They provide the energy.

PROTEINS
ABOUT 15% OF CALORIES

1) Help the body <u>grow</u> and <u>repair</u> itself.
2) Found in foods like <u>meat</u>, <u>fish</u>, <u>eggs</u>, <u>milk</u> and <u>soya beans</u>.
3) Made from chemicals called <u>amino acids</u> — there are two different types:
   a) <u>Non-essential Amino Acids</u> — your body can make these.
   b) <u>Essential Amino Acids</u> — your body can't make these, so you have to eat enough of them.

CARBOHYDRATES
ABOUT 55% OF CALORIES

<u>Provide energy</u>.
   a) <u>Simple Carbohydrates</u> (e.g. <u>sugar</u>). In <u>sweets</u>, <u>jam</u> and <u>cakes</u>. You shouldn't eat too much of these.
   b) <u>Complex Carbohydrates</u> (e.g. <u>starch</u>). In <u>bread</u>, <u>pasta</u>, <u>rice</u>, <u>potatoes</u> and <u>cereals</u>. These should be the biggest part of any meal.

FATS
ABOUT 30% OF CALORIES

Provide <u>energy</u> and keep us <u>warm</u>. Contain chemicals called <u>fatty acids</u>.
   a) <u>Saturated</u> Fatty Acids (Saturates). Found mainly in <u>animal products</u>.
   b) <u>Monosaturated</u> Fatty Acids (Monounsaturates). Found in many foods, like <u>olive oil</u>.
   c) <u>Polyunsaturated</u> Fatty Acids (Polyunsaturates). Found in some margarines and <u>oils</u>, and oily fish.

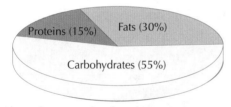

Proteins (15%) · Fats (30%) · Carbohydrates (55%)

About how much of each nutrient we should eat (by <u>calorie intake</u>, not weight)

1) <u>Carbohydrase enzymes</u> in the gut <u>break down</u> complex carbohydrates into simple ones (e.g. glucose), which then enter the <u>bloodstream</u>.
2) Some of the glucose is used <u>directly</u> for energy around the body.
3) The rest is converted to <u>glycogen</u> and stored in the <u>liver</u> and <u>muscles</u> until needed.

You need Small Amounts of *Vitamins* and *Minerals* too

VITAMINS

1) Help your <u>bones</u>, <u>teeth</u> and <u>skin</u> to grow.
2) Needed for many of the body's <u>chemical reactions</u>.

A) FAT-SOLUBLE VITAMINS

Can be <u>stored</u> in the body:
   a) <u>Vitamin A</u> — handy for <u>growth</u> and <u>night vision</u>, and found in vegetables, eggs and liver.
   b) <u>Vitamin D</u> — handy for <u>strong bones</u>, so you don't get <u>rickets</u>. Made by the skin in <u>sunshine</u>, but also found in milk, fish, liver and eggs.

B) WATER-SOLUBLE VITAMINS

<u>Can't be stored</u>, so you need to eat them regularly:
   a) <u>Vitamin C</u> — good for your <u>skin</u>, <u>gums</u> and <u>connective tissue</u>; you get <u>scurvy</u> without it. Found in fruit and veg. — especially citrus fruit like oranges and lemons.

With a properly balanced diet, you <u>don't need</u> vitamin supplements.

MINERALS

1) Needed for healthy <u>bones</u> and <u>teeth</u>, and to build other tissues.
2) Trace elements are minerals you only need a <u>little bit</u> of.

3) Minerals help in various <u>chemical reactions</u> in the body.
   a) <u>Calcium</u> — needed for strong <u>bones</u> and <u>teeth</u>, but also for <u>muscle contraction</u>. Lots in green vegetables, milk, cheese and some fish.
   b) <u>Iron</u> — handy for <u>haemoglobin</u> in red blood cells; you get <u>anaemia</u> without it. There's tons in liver, beans and green vegetables.
   c) <u>Iodine</u> — needed for <u>thyroid hormones</u>; you get <u>goitre</u> without it (swollen thyroid gland in neck). Found in sea food, and vegetables grown in iodine-rich soils.

Scurvy, rickets — even the names sound horrible...
Learn this page a nutrient at a time and it won't seem so bad...

Diet and Nutrition

You need to get the right balance of food, just like with anything else in life.
The trouble is, getting the balance right can be a bit tricky...

Water and Dietary Fibre are just as Important

Only protein, carbohydrate, fat, vitamins and minerals are really nutrients. But they're definitely not the only things you need. You'd have pretty major problems without these two...

WATER

1) Water's needed in loads of chemical reactions in the body. It's also lost in your breath, sweat, urine and faeces.

2) If you don't drink enough to replace what your body uses or loses you'll become dehydrated, and you won't perform as well.

3) If you drink too much, your kidneys will produce more urine to get rid of the excess.

DIETARY FIBRE

1) Fibre's not a nutrient either, but you need it to keep your digestive system working properly.

2) There's lots of fibre in fruit and vegetables — another good reason to eat loads of them.

A Balanced Diet — all the Nutrients in the Right Amounts

1) A balanced diet is one that contains all the nutrients you need in the right amounts for good health.

2) A good way to achieve this is to eat a varied diet with plenty of fruit and vegetables, but not too much fat.

3) People often talk about food groups. Including food from each group below can help you to get a balanced diet (though the last two groups aren't essential).

Bread, Nuts, Cereals, Pulses, Potatoes

Fruit and Vegetables

Meat and Fish

Dairy Foods

Eat Different Diets for Different Sports

Different sports place different demands on the body. That's why top athletes eat specific foods.

1) WEIGHTLIFTERS / SPRINTERS
Need muscle power, so they'll need lots of protein for muscle growth.

2) GYMNASTS
Need to be strong, but small and light. They need a good balance of carbohydrates, proteins and fats.

3) MARATHON RUNNERS
Need endurance over long periods, so they should get plenty of carbohydrates.

Organise Your Meals Around Activities

It's important to eat at the right times if you want to perform well at sport.

BEFORE AN ACTIVITY
Top athletes increase carbohydrate intake a few days before an event. This increases the amount of glycogen stored in the muscles, giving them plenty of energy. It's called carbohydrate loading.

DURING AN ACTIVITY
You shouldn't eat while exercising — your digestive system may not be able to cope. But you should drink to replace lost fluid.

AFTER AN ACTIVITY
Continue replacing lost fluid, but don't eat immediately. After a couple of hours, you should start eating to replace used energy.

Don't eat while exercising — being sick slows you down...
Lots to learn here, I'm afraid. But then diet is vital to performance in sport. Better read it all again...

Energy

All this energy lark's pretty straightforward really. Eat <u>as many</u> calories as you use up and you'll stay the <u>same weight</u>. Well, okay, maybe there's a <u>little more</u> to it than that...

Fats, Carbohydrates and Proteins Give You Energy

Fats, carbohydrates and proteins give us <u>energy</u> — the amount of energy is the <u>energy value</u>.

The energy needed to keep the <u>heart beating</u> and the <u>body breathing</u> (and for all the other processes that occur when you're completely at rest) is the <u>Basal Metabolic Rate</u> — or <u>BMR</u>.

Energy value is measured in <u>kilojoules</u> (kJ) or <u>kilocalories</u> (kcal) — but people usually say calories instead of kilocalories.

TOTAL ENERGY NEEDED = BMR + ENERGY USED TO WORK, PLAY ETC.

Each person has an <u>optimum weight</u>. This <u>varies</u> greatly depending on <u>height</u>, <u>shape</u>, <u>age</u> and <u>gender</u>. Moving <u>too far</u> from your optimum weight can reduce your <u>performance</u> and damage you <u>health</u>.

If you <u>eat more</u> than you <u>need</u>, the extra energy is stored as <u>adipose tissue</u> (i.e. <u>fat</u>) — and you <u>gain</u> weight.

Eating too much can lead to <u>obesity</u>, which is when someone has at least <u>20% more body fat</u> than the norm for their height and build. Obesity places a lot of <u>strain</u> on the <u>heart</u> and <u>muscles</u>.

If you <u>eat less</u> than you <u>need</u>, your body uses its reserves of <u>adipose tissue</u>, and you <u>lose</u> weight.

<u>Anorexia</u> is a <u>mental illness</u>. Sufferers refuse to eat and become dangerously thin. They often have a <u>distorted image</u> of their own body — still thinking they need to lose weight.

Weight Control — Exercise and a Balanced Diet

Many people try to lose weight by just <u>cutting down</u> on the <u>calories</u> — but that <u>rarely works</u>. <u>Just eating less</u> of the same thing but doing nothing else different <u>isn't the best way</u> to lose weight.

There are <u>two keys to losing weight</u>, and it works much better with both <u>together</u>:

1) Eat a more <u>balanced diet</u> — it's especially important not to overdo the <u>fat</u>. This might involve making a <u>permanent change</u> to the types of food you eat.

2) Get plenty of <u>exercise</u>. This bit's really important — partly because you'll <u>use up</u> <u>calories</u> exercising, but mainly because it'll <u>increase</u> your <u>basal metabolic rate (BMR)</u>, so you'll <u>use up more calories</u> when <u>resting</u> too.

Exercise also <u>suppresses the appetite</u>, so you won't want to eat as much.

BODY COMPOSITION IS A MEASURE OF BODY FAT — IT'S THE PERCENTAGE OF YOUR WEIGHT THAT'S FAT.

Being too fat OR too thin is bad for you...

Your Basal Metabolic Rate shows how much energy you need — it's like a car's miles per gallon. Remember that exercise can increase your BMR, so you burn more calories for free — neat. Learn how to lose weight sensibly with a balanced diet, combined with a good level of exercise...

Energy

Massive Phil, the weightlifter, will need loads more calories than little aunty Doris, who's only exercise is a stroll to the bingo hall on a Thursday. <u>Different people</u> need different amounts of <u>energy</u>...

Different People Need Different Amounts of Food

You need to know how different factors affect <u>how much food</u> people need.

1) AGE —
If you're <u>growing</u>, you need to eat more. Adults generally need less food.

2) LIFESTYLE —
An <u>office worker</u> needs less food than a <u>builder</u>.

4) SIZE & SEX —
The <u>bigger</u> you are, the more food you need — and <u>men</u> usually need more food than <u>women</u> for a given size.

3) SPORTS PLAYED —
Eat more if you play <u>strenuous sports</u>.

Glucose can be Converted into Energy in Two Ways

<u>Respiration</u> is the process that takes place in living cells to <u>release energy</u> from <u>food</u> molecules. There are <u>two kinds</u> of respiration — <u>aerobic</u> and <u>anaerobic</u>. They both convert <u>glucose into energy</u>. Which one the body uses depends on the <u>intensity</u> of the activity:

AEROBIC RESPIRATION — <u>with oxygen</u>

1) During <u>aerobic</u> activity, your heart and lungs supply your muscles with <u>plenty of oxygen</u>.

GLUCOSE + OXYGEN → CARBON DIOXIDE + WATER + ENERGY

2) You <u>breathe out</u> the <u>carbon dioxide</u> through your lungs, while the <u>water</u> is lost as <u>sweat</u>, <u>urine</u>, or in the <u>air</u> you breathe out.

3) As long as your muscles are supplied with <u>enough oxygen</u>, you can do aerobic exercise — so this is used for <u>long periods</u> of exercise.

This is how **marathon runners** get their energy.

ANAEROBIC RESPIRATION — <u>without oxygen</u>

1) During <u>anaerobic</u> activity, your muscles are <u>not</u> supplied with <u>enough oxygen</u>.

GLUCOSE (NO OXYGEN) → LACTIC ACID + ENERGY

2) This <u>lactic acid</u> builds up if there's a <u>shortage of oxygen</u> (this shortage of oxygen is called an <u>oxygen debt</u>).

3) Lactic acid is a <u>mild poison</u> and its build-up soon makes your muscles feel <u>tired</u> — so this is used for <u>short</u>, <u>strenuous</u> activities.

This is how **sprinters** get their energy.

Respiration — two types for the price of one...

Nothing's ever simple, is it? You'd think they could agree on one way to convert glucose to energy, but can they? No. Well, actually it's probably just as well we can do anaerobic respiration — otherwise we wouldn't have the energy to sprint to safety when we're chased by stampeding bison or angry teachers...

Endurance

How long your muscles can work for depends on your endurance — you need to know about the two kinds of endurance.

Muscular Endurance is Linked to Strength

You've got muscular endurance if your muscles can keep exerting a lot of force for a long time. Middle-distance runners have good muscular endurance — they run fast, but for quite a long time.

1) When your muscles can't work properly any more, your arms and legs start to feel heavy or weak, and muscle fatigue sets in.

2) Slow-twitch muscle fibres get tired less quickly — so it's easier to improve your muscular endurance if you've got loads of slow-twitch fibres.

To improve muscular endurance, you need to get stronger. Weight training is a good way to do this.

Cardiovascular Endurance is Linked to Heart and Lungs

Cardiovascular (CV) endurance (or CV fitness) is how good you are at keeping your muscles supplied with oxygen. This is the job of your heart and lungs.

1. As your muscles work harder, they need more oxygen — so your breathing and heart rate get faster to move more oxygen around the body.

2. The more efficient your cardiovascular system, the slower your pulse rate will be (either resting or exercising), and the quicker it will return to normal after you've been exercising.

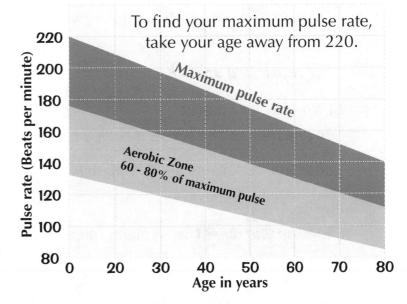

To find your maximum pulse rate, take your age away from 220.

Maximum pulse rate

Aerobic Zone
60 - 80% of maximum pulse

Pulse rate (Beats per minute)

Age in years

To improve your CV endurance, you have to work your heart and lungs hard for at least 15 minutes. Make sure your pulse is in the aerobic or target zones. Then your VO_2 will be between 55% and 75% of your VO_2 Max (see p15).

Learn about endurance — if you can take it...

Don't get muscular endurance confused with strength. Someone who can lift an incredibly heavy weight once doesn't necessarily have muscular endurance — but if they can lift it up and down for ten minutes, then they do have it. And make sure you can calculate target zones — they're important...

Warm-Up and Worked Exam Questions

Warm-up Questions

1) What is obesity?
2) What food group is usually the main provider of energy?
3) Name a good source of Vitamin C?
4) Apart from eating a better diet, what else could you do to lose weight?
5) Which two components of the body are most important in cardiovascular endurance?
6) Write two chemical word equations to show what happens in aerobic and anaerobic respiration.

Worked Exam Questions

You know what you have to do — carefully read through the worked examples, and then head over on to the next page for some exam-style practice questions.

1   Answer these questions about diet and nutrition.

a)   List the three main food types that provide the body with energy.

Carbohydrates, proteins and fats.

(3 marks)

b)   Explain the importance of the following substances in a person's diet:

i) Protein

For repair and growth.

ii) Vitamins and Minerals

To ensure healthy bones, teeth, skin and other tissues and to help in chemical reactions that happen in the body.

iii) Fibre

To keep the digestive system functioning properly.

(3 marks)

2   When training to improve cardiovascular endurance, you should train in your aerobic zone. Explain how the limits of your target heart rate range for the aerobic zone are calculated.

Maximum heart rate = 220 – your age

Training zone minimum = 60% of maximum heart rate

Training zone maximum = 80% of maximum heart rate

(3 marks)

Exam Questions

1   Chris and Val are both serious athletes. Chris is a weightlifter and Val is a marathon
     runner. They have both adapted their diets to suit their chosen sport.

   a)   Describe how their diets might differ.

     ....

     ....
     (2 marks)

   b)   Explain the process by which Val's body converts glucose into energy during her
          marathon. Write a chemical word equation showing the process.

     ....

     ....

     ....
     (3 marks)

2   a)   Explain the term "Basal Metabolic Rate".

     ....
     (1 mark)

   b)   What factors affect how much food a person requires?

     ....

     ....

     ....
     (3 marks)

3   a)   Name the by-product produced by anaerobic respiration.

     ....
     (1 mark)

   b)   Describe the conditions under which anaerobic respiration occurs and explain how
          its by-product affects performance.

     ....

     ....

     ....
     (2 marks)

Strength, Speed and Power

Strength, speed and power are closely linked — but they're all a bit different.
Here's what they actually are, and why they're needed...

Static, *Explosive* and *Dynamic* Strength

STATIC STRENGTH

1) You use static strength to exert force on an immovable object.
2) Muscles stay the same length, so there's not much movement.
3) Useful in arm-wrestling and a rugby scrum.

EXPLOSIVE STRENGTH

1) You use explosive strength to exert force in one very short, but very fast movement.
2) Closely linked to power.
3) Useful for the javelin or high jump.

DYNAMIC STRENGTH

1) You use dynamic strength to apply force repeatedly over a long time.
2) Linked to endurance.
3) Useful for doing loads of press-ups or cycling.

Most sports need all three kinds of strength — but they're usually not all equally important.

Speed Means *Reacting* and *Moving*

— REACTION TIME—
This is the time it takes you to respond to something. It could be a starter's gun, or a pass in football.

For speed, you need:
1) Fast reaction times,
2) Fast movement times.

—MOVEMENT TIME—
And this is the time it takes you to carry out a certain movement — e.g. a 100 m sprint, or a shot at goal.

You can increase your speed by training, but certain factors limit how successful you can be...

1 INHERITED CHARACTERISTICS
If you're born with a lot of fast-twitch muscle fibres, it's easier to increase your speed.

2 BODY SHAPE & SIZE
Your bone structure, weight, and muscle size put limits on how much you can increase your speed.

3 DURATION OF EVENT
It's just not possible to run flat-out forever — everybody slows down pretty soon. For longer distances, it's better to improve your endurance.

Increase speed by increasing your strength, or by improving your action — e.g. improve your tennis serve or golf swing.

Power Means *Speed* and *Strength* Together

Power is speed and strength combined — and there's a strong link between power and explosive strength. Most sports need power for some things — even ones like golf, where it's not obvious.

SPORT	YOU NEED POWER TO...
Football	...shoot
Golf	...drive
Table tennis	...smash
Tennis	...serve and smash
Cricket	...bowl fast and bat

Coordination and balance also help generate power — it's not just strength you need.

If your reactions are slow, it doesn't matter how fast you can move...

Another page with lots on it. The names of the different kinds of strength give you clues about the differences between them. And power's just a combination of speed and strength, so there's not really anything massively different in the last bit of the page. Make sure all this stuff is in your head.

Flexibility

Flexibility, suppleness, mobility — they're all the <u>same thing</u>. They're all to do with <u>how far</u> your joints move — and this depends on the <u>type of joint</u> and the 'stretchiness' of the <u>muscles</u> around it.

Flexibility has Many **Benefits**

It's often forgotten about, but <u>suppleness</u> is dead useful for any sport. Here's why...

1) STRETCHES GET YOU READY TO WORK

Stretching is a good way to <u>warm up</u> and get your body <u>ready to work</u>.

2) BETTER PERFORMANCE

You <u>can't</u> do some sports without being flexible — gymnastics, for example.

Flexibility makes you more <u>efficient</u> in other sports like swimming or hurdling — so you use <u>less energy</u>.

3) FEWER INJURIES

If you're flexible, you're less likely to <u>pull</u> or <u>strain</u> a muscle or <u>stretch too far</u> and injure yourself.

4) BETTER POSTURE

More flexibility means a better <u>posture</u> and <u>fewer aches</u> and <u>pains</u>.

Bad posture can lead to permanent <u>deformity</u> of the spine, as well as <u>straining</u> the abdominal muscles and back. It can also impair <u>breathing</u> — another way that flexibility affects performance.

> <u>Stretching</u> after exercising helps prevent <u>muscle soreness</u>.

Work Towards **All-Round** Flexibility

Flexibility in these <u>joints</u> is especially important because they're used all the time in <u>sport</u>:

For more about fitness testing, see pages 67 & 68.

> **BACK**
> <u>Most</u> movements need flexibility here. It's often <u>injured</u> because not many people have supple backs.

> **LEGS**
> Flexibility at the <u>knee</u> and <u>ankle</u> is important for <u>running</u> or <u>kicking</u>. Most people are pretty supple here through walking.

> **HIP**
> Anything involving <u>raising</u> or <u>lowering a leg</u> needs you to bend at the <u>hip</u>. Not many people are flexible here. It's a good place to <u>test</u> flexibility.

> **SHOULDERS & ARMS**
> Flexibility here helps with a lot of sports — like <u>throwing</u> and <u>swimming</u>. Most people stretch these joints <u>getting dressed</u> in the morning.

> Strength training can <u>limit flexibility</u> — so do plenty of <u>stretching</u> exercises as well.

Active or **Passive Stretches** Improve Flexibility

Flexibility's a good thing, so you should know how to <u>improve</u> it. In a nutshell, you need to move the joint <u>past</u> where it would <u>normally go</u>, but there are <u>two ways</u> to do that:

ACTIVE STRETCHING

1) <u>You</u> do the work of stretching your muscles — <u>slowly</u> and <u>gently</u>.

2) If it <u>hurts</u>, or if your muscles start to <u>shake</u>, <u>ease up</u>.

3) <u>Don't bounce</u> into a stretch because you can <u>tear</u> muscle fibres.

PASSIVE STRETCHING

1) A <u>partner</u> does the work of stretching your muscles.

2) Tell him or her straight away if you feel any <u>pain</u>.

I wish I could do passive revision...

Knowing the benefits of flexibility will be important in the exam — but also make sure you know the dangers of stretching incorrectly. And don't be confused by the three different names for flexibility — suppleness and mobility are exactly the same thing. Get learning, and have fun.

Age

A person's <u>age</u> will affect how well they can play most sports. Some sports are too <u>physically demanding</u> for older people to compete with younger players. But this <u>isn't true</u> of <u>all sports</u>...

Age Affects Performance in Sport

Age affects performance in loads of different ways. Make sure you know how.

STRENGTH
1) You don't reach your <u>maximum strength</u> until you're fully grown — usually at about <u>20</u>.
2) In your 20s and 30s, it's still <u>easy</u> to <u>build more muscle</u>.
3) After this, <u>protein levels</u> and <u>muscle mass fall</u>, strength <u>declines</u> and it's <u>harder</u> to <u>build muscle</u>.

OXYGEN CAPACITY
This <u>falls</u> as you get older — <u>less oxygen</u> can be taken to the muscles.

REACTION TIMES
Your reactions get <u>slower</u> as you get older.

INJURY & DISEASE
1) Older people are more likely to <u>injure</u> themselves.
2) It takes <u>longer</u> for an older person to <u>recover</u> from an injury.
3) Older people generally suffer more from <u>diseases</u> — cancer and heart disease, for example.

FLEXIBILITY
1) People are most <u>flexible</u> in their <u>teens</u> (or earlier).
2) After the age of about <u>30</u>, most people have started to become <u>less flexible</u>.

EXPERIENCE
1) Experience is often a <u>vital factor</u> in sport.
2) As you get older, you gain more experience.

This is why there are often <u>age divisions</u> in competitions.
An 8-year-old can't compete fairly in <u>most sports</u> against a 14-year-old.
Similarly, people of 50 can't usually compete against people of 25.

Older competitors — low on speed, but high on experience...

Another page with lots on it that you just have to remember. Test yourself. Cover the page up and see if you can write down the ways that age affects performance. And don't just learn it once — test yourself regularly before the exam so you don't forget. It's the only way.

Age and Gender

Performance is affected by <u>gender</u> as well as age. Men and women rarely compete against each other, because of their <u>physical differences</u>. But for some sports, age and gender don't matter as much.

Age *Doesn't Matter* for Some Sports

Lots of sports are thought of as 'for old people' or 'for young people'. This isn't always <u>fair</u>.

If a sport depends on <u>strength</u> or <u>endurance</u> (e.g. weightlifting or marathon running), older people will have a <u>disadvantage</u> — but for less strenuous sports (e.g. bowls), this <u>doesn't have to be true</u>.

> You can <u>control</u> some of the effects of <u>ageing</u> (e.g. stretching can slow down the loss of flexibility), but <u>not others</u>.

Gender can affect Performance

As well as separating young and old, competitions usually split men and women. Here's why...

MEN & WOMEN HAVE DIFFERENT BODIES

1) Men generally have a <u>longer</u>, <u>heavier</u> bone structure.
2) Women have a <u>wider</u>, <u>flatter pelvis</u> (which is better for childbearing).
3) Women generally have <u>more body fat</u> than men.
4) The <u>menstrual cycle</u> can affect performance.

GIRLS MATURE EARLIER THAN BOYS

1) Girls reach physical maturity at <u>16 or 17</u>.
2) Boys don't mature until about <u>20</u>.

MEN ARE GENERALLY STRONGER

Men generally have <u>bigger muscles</u>, due to higher <u>testosterone</u> levels.
On average, men are <u>stronger</u> and <u>faster</u> than women.

Women are generally more flexible.

WOMEN ARE GENERALLY MORE FLEXIBLE

This is partly because they've got <u>less muscle</u>.
In sports like <u>gymnastics</u> and <u>figure skating</u>, women can often do moves that men can't.

Women are <u>discriminated</u> against in some sports — they get less <u>prize money</u>, and their events have a lower <u>profile</u>. *See page 88 for more info.*

I always thought that girls were more mature...

It's often impractical for men and women to compete against each other — there's just too big a difference in speed and strength. That's not to say that men are better — just different. Pairs figure skating is a good example — each partner plays a different role, but they're both just as important...

Somatotype

<u>Somatotype</u> means the basic <u>shape</u> of your body. Your somatotype can have a big effect on your <u>suitability</u> for a particular sport. Being the <u>right shape</u> is <u>no guarantee</u> of success, but it <u>helps</u>.

Somatotypes are Body Shapes

There are <u>three</u> basic somatotypes — <u>ectomorph</u>, <u>mesomorph</u> and <u>endomorph</u>. Everyone's body shape can be described by three numbers from <u>1 to 7</u> — one for each of the 3 basic somatotypes. Think of these basic somatotypes as <u>extremes</u> — at the <u>corners</u> of a triangular graph.

REMEMBER
ENDOMORPH — Dumpy,
MESOMORPH — Muscular,
ECTOMORPH — Thin.

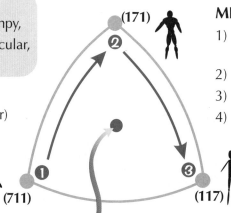

MESOMORPH (2nd number)
1) <u>Wide shoulders</u> and relatively <u>narrow hips</u>.
2) <u>Muscular</u> body.
3) <u>Strong</u> arms and thighs.
4) <u>Not</u> much body <u>fat</u>.

ENDOMORPH (1st number)
1) <u>Wide hips</u> but relatively <u>narrow shoulders</u>.
2) A lot of <u>fat</u> on body, arms and legs.
3) <u>Ankles</u> and <u>wrists</u> are relatively <u>slim</u>.

A score of <u>444</u> (for Mr Average) would be in the <u>middle</u> of the graph.

ECTOMORPH (3rd number)
1) <u>Narrow</u> shoulders, hips and chest.
2) <u>Not</u> much <u>muscle or fat</u>.
3) <u>Long</u>, <u>thin</u> arms and legs.
4) <u>Thin face</u> and <u>high forehead</u>.

Everyone is a <u>mixture</u> of all three basic body types — but people who play sport at a very <u>high level</u> tend to get high <u>mesomorph</u> scores, since <u>strength</u> is often important in sport.

Different Somatotypes Suit Different Sports

Particular sports are usually more <u>suited</u> to certain body types. So having a <u>high number</u> for the right body type gives you a <u>natural advantage</u>:

<u>Sumo wrestlers</u> need strength, weight, and a low centre of gravity — strong <u>endomorphic</u> and <u>mesomorphic</u> features.

<u>High jumpers</u> need to be tall and light, but with powerful muscles — <u>ectomorphic</u> and <u>mesomorphic</u> features.

Ideal somatotypes for different sports.

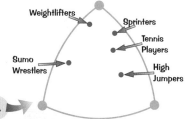

ENDOMORPHS
Suited to activities like <u>wrestling</u> and <u>shot-putting</u>.

MESOMORPHS
Suited to activities like the <u>decathlon</u>, <u>swimming</u>, <u>gymnastics</u> and <u>bodybuilding</u>.

ECTOMORPHS
Suited to activities like <u>long-distance running</u> and <u>high jumping</u>.

Here's a nice bunch of fancy words for you to learn...

Be sure to learn the word somatotype. It's a fancy word — but all it means is somebody's shape. And remember, nearly everybody is a mixture of the three basic body types. Learn the names well — it'd be a bad mistake to get the three basic somatotypes confused. Get your learning hat on.

Sport and Personality

Your personality can influence the types of sport you prefer. If you're a quiet sort of person, you'll probably like different sports from someone who's louder. Get learning this stuff.

People with Different Personalities Prefer Different Sports

You can describe people's personalities by saying how extroverted or introverted they are. Some people can be called extroverts, and some called introverts. But this can be misleading, because no one is completely extroverted or introverted — they're just closer to one or the other.

This diagram shows the effect that personality has on people's choice of sport.

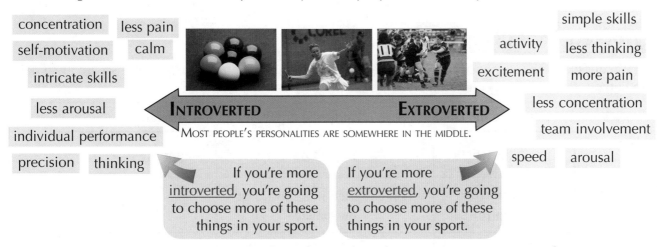

concentration   less pain
self-motivation   calm
intricate skills
less arousal
individual performance
precision   thinking

INTROVERTED   EXTROVERTED

MOST PEOPLE'S PERSONALITIES ARE SOMEWHERE IN THE MIDDLE.

simple skills
activity   less thinking
excitement   more pain
less concentration
team involvement
speed   arousal

If you're more introverted, you're going to choose more of these things in your sport.

If you're more extroverted, you're going to choose more of these things in your sport.

These are only general rules — you'll be able to find loads of exceptions.

Aggression Has To Be Controlled

Aggression can have good and bad effects. It's good if it's kept under control — but bad if it means you break the rules or injure an opponent. There are two types of aggression.

INDIRECT AGGRESSION
Indirect aggression means hitting objects (like a tennis ball or cricket ball).

DIRECT AGGRESSION
Direct aggression is when there is actual physical contact between two competitors — like in boxing or rugby.

Aggression in some athletes — like swimmers — could be just a fierce determination to succeed. But for athletes like boxers, the aggression is a bit more obvious.

Golfers are aggressive towards a ball, so they can hit it a long way.

Tennis players may hit the ball very hard towards their opponent.

Boxers actually try to harm their opponent.

Aggression in sport must be controlled, otherwise it can make your performance worse.

Learn about aggression — LEARN IT OR ELSE!
You'll need to learn the kinds of things that introverts and extroverts prefer — time to cover the page again and see how much of it you can write down. Pick a couple of friends — an introvert and an extrovert — and associate the different qualities with them. It makes it a bit more relevant to you.

Warm-Up and Worked Exam Questions

Warm-up Questions

1) Which muscle fibre type is best for speed?
2) Power is a combination of what two things?
3) What are the three different types of strength?
4) List three components of fitness that age has a negative effect on.
5) What does "somatotype" describe?
6) List three sports that you would expect an introverted person to prefer?

Worked Exam Questions

These questions have the answers on them — trust me, they won't do in your exam — so use them now to find out how to answer questions well.

1 a) Complete the table below to identify the different types of strength.

Type of Strength	Definition	Sporting Example
Explosive Strength	Force exerted in a short, fast movement	Javelin
Dynamic Strength	Force applied repeatedly over a long time	Press-ups
Static Strength	Force exerted on an immovable object	Arm wrestle/rugby scrum

(6 marks)

b) Identify three benefits of having good flexibility.

Reduced risk of injury, better performance, better posture.

(3 marks)

2 a) Identify one characteristic of body shape for each of the following somatotypes.

i) Endomorph *Wide hips*
ii) Mesomorph *Muscular*
iii) Ectomorph *Thin*

There are more possible answers you could give.

(3 marks)

b) "Extroverts are more likely to participate in team sports."
Give two reasons why this may be true.

Extroverts are more sociable, and tend to enjoy the speed and excitement commonly associated with team sports.

Answer the question. Don't just say what extroverts like — say what they like about team sports.

(2 marks)

Exam Questions

1   Complete the table below to identify the components of fitness required by different sports.

Fitness Component	Sport	Why component is needed
Strength	Rugby	
	Tennis	To serve and smash
	Sprinting	To win the race
Flexibility	Gymnastics	

(4 marks)

2   Give three physical factors that make it inappropriate for men and women to compete against each other in most sports.

....

....

....

(3 marks)

3   a)   Briefly describe the three basic somatotypes.

....

....

....

(3 marks)

b)   Give an example of a sport that each somatotype would be suited to.

....

....

....

(3 marks)

Hygiene

Hygiene's pretty important. Without it, the world would be a dirtier, smellier, yuckier place. So you need to know what to keep clean, and what happens if you let it get smelly.

Hygiene Helps Keep You Healthy and Odour-Free

This is important for keeping yourself healthy, and also for staying popular with your friends. Your hygiene routine should include paying attention to:

WASHING
Have a regular shower or bath and dry yourself properly to avoid dirt and grime building up, B.O. (Body Odour), and infections.

TEETH
Brush your teeth at least twice a day, and get them checked over regularly by a dentist to avoid tooth decay, gum disease and bad breath — especially as you get older.

CLOTHES
Change your clothes often, and especially after playing sport, to avoid whiffy smells.

> **SWEAT**
> 1) When you exercise, your body produces sweat to help keep you cool.
> 2) Sweat is a mixture of water, salts, ammonia, and other waste products.
> 3) Sweat itself doesn't smell, but when bacteria on your skin start feeding on it, they start to get pretty whiffy.

Avoid Athlete's Foot and Verrucas by wearing Flip-Flops

Athlete's foot and verrucas are infections you can easily catch, but just as easily avoid.

ATHLETE'S FOOT — caused by a fungus
1) It's a fungus that grows between your toes and makes them itch.
2) You catch it through contact with infected socks, towels or changing room floors.
3) Avoid it by wearing flip-flops in shared changing rooms, always drying between your toes after washing them, and avoiding shoes or socks that make your feet sweat.
4) It can be treated with powder or ointment from the chemist.

VERRUCAS — caused by a virus
1) These are flat warts that grow on the bottom of your feet.
2) They're caused by a virus, are very easily caught, and are transmitted in the same way as athlete's foot.
3) Always wear flip-flops when sharing a changing room with other people.
4) They can be treated with ointment or pads from the chemist.

Bad Shoes Mean Bad Feet

Ill-fitting shoes can give your feet no end of trouble...

BLISTERS
1) These are usually caused by shoes which rub.
2) Don't burst a blister — it increases the risk of infection.
3) If it bursts on its own, keep it clean and dry.

BUNIONS
1) A bunion is an inflammation of the joint between your big toe and your foot.
2) Only surgery can get rid of these.

> The BBC of ill-fitting shoes: Blisters, Bunions & Corns

CORNS
1) These are hard pads of skin on your toes and feet.
2) You can get corn plasters from a chemist to get rid of them.

Blister | Bunion | Corn

The BBC — The British Bunioning Corporation...

Learn the important points for a hygiene routine, and how to avoid athlete's foot and verrucas.

Drugs

Doping, or taking drugs, is a big problem in sport. You'll need to know the different kinds of drugs that can be taken, what they do, and why they're banned in international competitions.

Alcohol and Tobacco are Legal but Harmful

Although alcohol and tobacco are legal, they're still drugs and can affect your performance badly.

ALCOHOL

1) Affects your coordination, speech and judgement,
2) Slows your reactions,
3) Makes your muscles get tired more quickly,
4) Eventually damages your liver, kidneys, heart, muscles, brain, and the digestive and immune systems.

SMOKING

1) Causes nose, throat and chest irritations,
2) Makes you short of breath,
3) Increases the risk of developing heart disease, lung cancer, bronchitis, and other diseases.

Small amounts of alcohol don't do too much harm, but every cigarette does damage.

Performance Enhancing Drugs — Remember SNAPD

These performance enhancing drugs are banned by the International Olympic Committee (IOC).

STIMULANTS

1) Speed up your reactions and increase aggression.
2) Make you feel less pain.

But...

1) Feeling less pain can make an athlete train too hard.
2) They can lead to high blood pressure, heart and liver problems, and strokes.
3) They're addictive.

NARCOTIC ANALGESICS

1) Kill pain — so injuries and fatigue don't affect performance so much.

But...

1) They're addictive, with unpleasant withdrawal symptoms.
2) Feeling less pain can make an athlete train too hard.
3) They can lead to constipation and low blood pressure.

An easy way to remember which drugs are banned by the IOC is to remember SNAPD.

S — Stimulants
N — Narcotic analgesics
A — Anabolic agents
P — Peptide hormones
D — Diuretics

ANABOLIC AGENTS
(or **steroids**)

1) Increase muscle size.
2) Allow athletes to train harder.

But...

1) They cause high blood pressure, heart disease, infertility and cancer.
2) Women may grow facial and body hair, and their voices may deepen.

PEPTIDE HORMONES

1) Most have a similar effect to anabolic steroids.
2) EPO (Erythropoietin) has a similar effect to blood doping (see next page).

But...

They can cause strokes and abnormal growth.

DIURETICS

1) Make you urinate, causing weight loss — important if you're competing in a certain weight division.
2) Can mask traces of other drugs in the body.

But...

They can cause cramp and dehydration.

A lot of these drugs were developed as medicines — but misuse does damage.

Drugs can damage athletes as well as help them...

Remember that alcohol generally makes you do everything more slowly — speak, react, think etc. And make sure you can write down what each of the different kinds of drugs actually do.

Drugs

There are other types of drug that people use to cheat — some of them quite <u>surprising</u>. Fortunately, there are <u>drug testing</u> procedures with severe <u>punishments</u> so mostly they won't get away with it.

B CALM Drugs are Restricted

The <u>International Olympic Committee</u> (IOC) <u>restricts</u> the use of these drugs — learn what they are.

BETA BLOCKERS

1) They're medicines that <u>lower the heart rate</u>, steady shaking hands and <u>reduce anxiety</u>.

2) They're <u>banned</u> in sports where they might give an advantage, such as <u>shooting</u>, <u>ski-jumping</u>, <u>snooker</u> and <u>bobsleigh</u>.

CORTICOSTEROIDS

1) They help <u>reduce pain</u> and <u>inflammation</u> from injuries.

2) They have some quite serious <u>side effects</u>, including diabetes, depression and bone weakness.

To remember the <u>restricted</u> drugs, remember B CALM.

ALCOHOL
It's sometimes used in snooker or shooting to <u>calm nerves</u>.

LOCAL ANAESTHETICS
They <u>reduce pain</u>, but might be allowed for medical purposes.

MARIJUANA
It has a similar effect to <u>alcohol</u>.

B — Beta blockers
C — Corticosteroids
A — Alcohol
L — Local anaesthetics
M — Marijuana

Dope Testing can happen at Any Time

There are strict <u>procedures</u> for drug testing. They protect athletes and mean results can be <u>double-checked</u>. If an athlete is found guilty, punishments can be <u>severe</u> — including lifetime bans.

THE TESTING PROCEDURE

1) Urine samples are divided into <u>two bottles</u> — the <u>A</u>- and <u>B-samples</u>.

2) The A-sample is tested. If drugs are found, the B-sample is tested to <u>double-check</u> the result.

3) <u>Refusing</u> to give a sample is as serious as <u>failing</u> a drugs test.

PUNISHMENTS FOR CHEATS

If an athlete is found <u>guilty</u> of taking banned drugs, they're <u>banned from competing</u> — possibly <u>forever</u>.

All of the testing takes place in <u>official labs</u> — and no one is supposed to know whose sample they're testing.

Blood Doping is Banned

Blood doping and 'physical manipulation' are also banned, since athletes get an <u>unfair advantage</u>.

BLOOD DOPING
Blood doping is used to <u>simulate high-altitude training</u> — without actually going to high altitude.

1) <u>Red blood cells</u> are <u>taken out</u> of an athlete — their body then <u>makes more</u> red blood cells to replace them.

2) Before a competition, the red blood cells are <u>injected back</u>, so that <u>more oxygen</u> can be carried round their body.

Possible <u>side effects</u> include allergic reactions, kidney damage, viruses (such as AIDS), and blocked capillaries.

PHYSICAL MANIPULATION
This includes interfering with a <u>urine sample</u> after it's been given.

B CALM — the exam's easy if you know this...
Make extra sure you know the difference between the B CALM drugs on this page and the SNAPD drugs on the previous page — SNAPD drugs are banned, but B CALM drugs are restricted.

Other Things That Affect Performance

There are also some other things that can affect your performance. They're not all things you can <u>control</u> — but they are all things you have to <u>know about</u> before you go into your exam.

Physiological Factors Affect Your *Body*

Things like lack of <u>sleep</u> or a <u>cold</u> can also affect performance. Be sure you know about these.

ILLNESS OR MEDICAL CONDITION

1 <u>Colds or flu</u> can make you <u>short of breath</u>, affect your <u>concentration</u>, and make you feel <u>weak</u>.
2 <u>Asthma</u> affects the <u>breathing</u>, but can be controlled.
3 <u>Hayfever</u> is an allergy to pollen from plants. It causes <u>sneezing</u>, and makes your <u>eyes water</u> and your <u>nose run</u>.
4 <u>Anaemia</u> is when you don't have enough <u>red blood cells</u> — or your red blood cells don't have enough <u>haemoglobin</u>. It can make you <u>short of breath</u> and <u>dizzy</u>.

STALENESS
Poor form and staleness can be caused by <u>overdoing things</u> — like exercising without enough <u>breaks</u>.

FATIGUE
When your body hasn't had time to <u>recover</u> from exercise, your performance can be affected.

LACK OF SLEEP
Without enough sleep, you <u>lose strength</u> and <u>concentration</u> more quickly.

MENSTRUATION
Women tend to perform better at certain stages of the <u>menstrual cycle</u>.

ABC is for *Agility*, *Balance* and *Coordination*

These <u>factors</u> can also affect performance. They're important — so you need to learn them.

AGILITY
When you can <u>change direction</u> and <u>body position</u> very quickly.

BALANCE
When you don't <u>wobble</u> or <u>fall over</u> easily.

COORDINATION
When you can move your body <u>precisely</u> and <u>smoothly</u> to <u>respond</u> to something.

There's no point being a strong, supple gymnast if you can't balance...
It's sad, but true, that even the best athletes can perform badly if there's something wrong with them. Illness is an obvious problem, but make sure you learn all the more obscure factors too. Don't forget about ABC either — these little things can make a massive difference to a competitor...

53

Other Things That Affect Performance

All sorts of factors can affect a competitor. These factors can be <u>external</u> as well as internal.
Conditions on the day are important.

External Factors can have an Effect

ENVIRONMENT/WEATHER/CLIMATE

1) <u>Hot</u> or <u>humid</u> weather can adversely affect your performance in a lot of sports.
   It's especially problematic for <u>endurance athletes</u>, like long-distance runners and cyclists.
   Competitors who <u>train</u> in hot climates tend to cope <u>better</u> with hot conditions when they compete.

2) In the same way, if it's <u>freezing cold</u>, you're likely to play many sports worse.
   <u>Cold muscles</u> don't perform as well as warm ones and are more <u>easily strained</u>.

3) <u>Wind</u> can also make playing sport more difficult. A strong <u>head-wind</u> can make running
   much harder. In games like tennis or rugby, the <u>ball</u> can be <u>blown off course</u>.

ALTITUDE

The air is <u>thinner</u> at higher altitudes, making athletes feel <u>short of breath</u>.
The body <u>adapts</u> to compensate for this over time. People who <u>live</u> or <u>train</u>
at <u>high altitude</u> perform better in many <u>endurance</u> events.

EQUIPMENT

The better your <u>equipment</u>, the better you're likely to perform. This is particularly true in sports like
<u>sailing</u> and <u>motor racing</u>, where choosing or designing the right equipment is part of the competition.

TECHNOLOGY

Technological developments in <u>equipment</u>, <u>materials</u> and <u>training</u> methods (e.g. using
video and computer technology) are pushing back the <u>bounds</u> of performance.

Other factors can affect performance too

Here are just a <u>few more things</u> to bear in mind when talking about performance.

PHYSICAL ABILITY

This is your <u>fitness</u> and <u>skill level</u>.
You need to learn skills and <u>practise</u>
to improve them and to <u>keep fit</u>.

SENSES

Sharp <u>eyesight</u> or a delicate
sense of <u>touch</u> can be important.

MENTAL ABILITY

When you play sport, you have to make <u>good decisions</u>.
A lot of it comes down to <u>practice</u> and <u>experience</u>.

EXPERIENCE

This is often vital in competitions.
Experienced competitors tend to make
<u>better decisions</u> and get <u>less nervous</u>.

MENTAL PREPARATION

<u>Relaxation techniques</u> can reduce anxiety and
help performers <u>focus</u> on the task at hand.
Mental <u>rehearsal</u> will also help preparation.

It's all in the mind — well some of it is, anyway...

Mental readiness has a big part to play in achieving optimum performance. Experience can be a real
help — experienced competitors can make the right decision quickly, because they've learnt from
previous competitions. This can compensate a bit for the physical disadvantages of being older.

Warm-Up and Worked Exam Questions

Warm-up Questions

1) List three things you should do to look after your own personal hygiene.
2) What can you do to avoid foot infections?
3) Why do some athletes take drugs?
4) How are athletes tested for drug use?
5) List five things that may affect performance.
6) Performance can be affected by physiological factors (the state your body is in) and sociological factors (the environment). What other type of factor can affect performance?

Worked Exam Questions

Work carefully through the questions below, making sure you understand them, then move onto the practice questions on the next page. It's not too late to have another flick through the last few pages.

1   a)   What is athlete's foot, how can you catch it and how can it be treated?

It's a fungus and can be caught from contact with infected socks, towels and floors. It can be treated with powder or cream.

Make sure you've answered all three parts of this question.

(3 marks)

b)   Identify three problems that can arise from ill-fitting shoes.

blisters, bunions, corns   *Remember — BBC.*

(3 marks)

2   Some athletes take anabolic steroids to improve their performance.
a)   Explain how steroids can improve performance.

They allow the athlete to train longer / harder without fatigue.

They help to build up muscle strength and size.

(2 marks)

b)   Identify two possible negative side effects from taking steroids.

Mood swings, high blood pressure, heart disease, infertility, cancer, facial and body hair on women, deeper voice in women.

Any two of these will get you the marks.

(2 marks)

3   Describe how the following may have an effect on your body.

a)   Cold or flu   *Shortness of breath, will tire more easily.*

b)   Asthma   *Breathing affected.*

c)   Hayfever   *Sneezing, runny eyes and nose.*

d)   Anaemia   *Shortness of breath, dizziness, fatigue.*

(4 marks)

Exam Questions

1   a)   What is a verruca?

....
(1 mark)

b)   How can they be avoided and treated?

....

....
(2 marks)

2   a)   Complete the table below to identify the effects of performance-enhancing drugs.

Name of Drug	Effect on Performance	Side Effects
Anabolic Steroids	ability to train longer, increased muscle size	
Stimulants		high blood pressure, heart and liver problems, strokes
	kill pain	constipation, low blood pressure
EPO (polypeptide hormones)		strokes, abnormal growth
Diuretics	weight loss caused by frequent urination	
Beta Blockers		addiction

(6 marks)

b)   Describe the process of blood doping which is used by some athletes to simulate the effects of high-altitude training.

....

....

....

....
(4 marks)

3   In nearly all sports, agility, balance and coordination are required to perform well.
Using a sport of your choice, explain why these three components are so important.

....

....

....
(3 marks)

Revision Summary for Section Two

That's it then — the end of another section. There's lots in it, but it's all stuff you need to know for the exam. You'll need to learn all the info about fitness — what it is and how things like diet, age, drugs and so on can affect it. Then there are the bits about health and hygiene. But don't panic — all you need to do is learn the facts, and then the exam will be easy. To test how much you know, and how much you still need to revise, try these questions — and keep revising until you know all the answers.

1) List seven factors that can affect someone's health.
2) Give a definition of general fitness.
3) As well as being generally fit, what six things do you need for specific fitness?
4) Name six factors that can affect fitness.
5) Name three types of people who should take things easy when they start to exercise.
6) Give two examples of how you can get more exercise by changing bad habits.
7) When you start to exercise, what changes 'kick in' to keep your muscles supplied with oxygen?
8) Which hormone helps cause the changes from Question 7?
9) What does 'shunting blood' mean?
10) What does your body do to cool you down when exercising?
11) Why do you still need lots of oxygen after you've finished exercising hard?
12) Describe the benefits of aerobic training.
13) What is hypertrophy?
14) About what percentage of your calories should come from proteins? Carbohydrates? Fats? What other nutrients do you need?
15) What are the two kinds of amino acids? What are the two kinds of carbohydrates? And the three kinds of fats?
16) Why do you need water-soluble vitamins regularly?
17) Why is having the right amount of water in your body so important? How does your body control your water balance?
18) Why is it important to eat fibre?
19) Describe what is meant by a balanced diet.
20) What are the two things you should do if you want to lose weight?
21) Name the two ways in which glucose can be converted into energy. When is each way used?
22) What are the three kinds of strength? What's the difference between strength and power?
23) Why is flexibility important for sport? How could you improve your flexibility?
24) List six ways in which age can affect performance at sport. How does gender affect performance?
25) Name the three basic somatotypes. How would you describe each of these somatotypes? Give an example of a sport that each somatotype is suited to.
26) Which kinds of sports do introverts and extroverts usually prefer?
27) Name three things you should definitely include in your hygiene routine.
28) What is athlete's foot? And what's a verruca? How would you avoid them?
29) Name three foot problems that you can get if your shoes don't fit properly.
30) What five kinds of drugs are banned by the IOC? What five kinds are restricted?
31) What is blood doping?
32) Name five physiological factors that can affect somebody's performance at sport.
33) Name 12 other factors that can affect performance (yes, 12 — a dozen).

Training Sessions

Training's <u>not</u> about running for as <u>long</u> as possible, or lifting the <u>heaviest</u> weights you can. There's much <u>more</u> to it than that — and you'll be asked about it in the exam, so get reading.

Always **Warm Up** First and **Cool Down** Afterwards

These are <u>vital</u> to every training session — make sure you know why:

WARM-UP — gradually gets your body <u>ready</u> for the training.

1) Increases the <u>temperature</u> of the body, and increases <u>blood flow</u> to the muscles — so they can do the work later on in the training.

2) <u>Stretches</u> the muscles, moves the joints and increases the <u>range of movement</u> — so you're ready for the work and less likely to <u>injure</u> yourself.

3) Concentrates the <u>mind</u> on the training.

> You should warm up your <u>cardiovascular system first</u>. Do some <u>gentle exercise</u>, like jogging, until you are <u>just out of breath</u>. Then <u>stretch</u>.

COOL-DOWN — gets your body back to normal.

1) Helps <u>repay the oxygen debt</u> in your muscles and <u>remove waste products</u> such as lactic acid.

2) Gets rid of the <u>extra blood</u> in your muscles, and so stops it <u>pooling</u> in your veins. Blood pooling can make you feel <u>dizzy</u> and <u>weak</u> if you stop exercising suddenly.

SPORT — The **Five Principles** of Training

S | **SPECIFICITY** — Every person will need a <u>different</u> training program — we're all different and we all do different things.

    1) Train the <u>right parts</u> of the body — there's <u>no point</u> making a weightlifter run 10 miles a day — it won't improve their weightlifting.

    2) Train to the <u>right level</u> — if someone's dead <u>unfit</u>, don't start them with a <u>5-mile swim</u>.

P | **PROGRESSION** — <u>Steadily increase</u> the amount of training that's done — but only when the body has <u>adapted</u> to the previous training.

O | **OVERLOAD** — You've got to make your body <u>work harder</u> than it normally would. You've got to <u>push yourself</u> beyond the <u>training threshold</u> (see page 59). It's the <u>only way</u> to get fitter. You can overload by increasing any of these <u>three</u>:

    1 Frequency of training (e.g. training more often),

    2 Intensity of training (e.g. lifting heavier weights),

    3 Time (duration) of training (e.g. training for 5 minutes longer each session).

R | **REVERSIBILITY** — Your <u>fitness level changes</u> all the time — and it will go down if you stop training. It takes much <u>longer to gain</u> fitness than to <u>lose fitness</u>.

T | **TEDIUM AVOIDANCE** — Use different ways of training to give variety and avoid boredom.

Learn SPORT — this is PE after all...

Warming up and cooling down is pretty obvious, and just needs learning, but the principles of training are much harder. Just remember that the principles begin with the letters in the word SPORT.

Training Sessions

The best training programmes aren't just thrown together at the last moment — they have to be <u>carefully planned</u>. All the stuff you need to know is here — get it all in your head.

Training should be *Interesting* as well as *Useful*

TRAINING — An exercise routine needs these <u>three things</u> to make it <u>interesting</u> and <u>useful</u>:

1) Loads of <u>different things</u> in each session — so you don't get <u>bored</u>.
2) Time to <u>warm up</u> and <u>cool down</u>.
3) Regular checking and <u>assessment</u> to make sure it's still <u>suitable</u> and good enough.

A *Training Programme* must *Suit* the Person it's for

The programme must <u>suit</u> the person it's for — so you've got to find out about them.
Good <u>questions</u> to ask them include...

What exercise do you like?

Do you live near any sports facilities?

What sports do you play?

Do you have any injuries?

How old are you?

What exercise do you find boring?

How fit are you now?

Do you have any health problems?

Why do you want to get fitter?

There are *Four Stages* of Training for *Competition*

Your training should be different for each <u>stage</u> of the year.

1 OUT-OF-SEASON PREPARATION —
Eat plenty of carbohydrates, and do lots of aerobic and strength training.

2 PRE-SEASON PREPARATION —
Do anaerobic, aerobic and skills training — plus some extra strength training.

3 COMPETITION —
Compete regularly, while maintaining your fitness and getting enough rest.
Training can be planned so that you 'peak' at the right time (e.g. for key competitions).

4 RECUPERATION —
Recover from the strain of competition through rest and relaxation.

Recuperation — my favourite stage of training...

Making a training programme that fits the person it's meant for is a really important idea to get into your head. Remember to consider not only their age and fitness, but also the reasons they want to get fit. Is it just to lose weight, or are they aiming to play sport at a high level? It really matters.

Training Sessions

Training programmes <u>vary a lot</u>, but they all need to take into account certain <u>principles</u>.
Here's what you need to know to plan a really useful programme...

Programmes can be Planned using FITT

F = FREQUENCY of activity — how <u>often</u> you should exercise.
E.g. if you just want to stay <u>healthy</u> you should exercise for at least <u>20 minutes twice a week</u>. If you're training to get into the national gymnastics team, you might need to train for a <u>few hours 5 or 6 days a week</u>.
If you do a hard workout you should give your body at least <u>24 hours</u> rest before you exercise again.

I = INTENSITY of activity — how <u>hard</u> you should exercise.
E.g. if you wanted to <u>lose weight</u> you should raise your heart rate to about <u>75%</u> of your <u>maximum safe heart rate</u> for 20 minutes or over. (<u>Max heart rate is about 220 minus your age in years</u>.) If you're training to improve your speed and stamina, you'll need to raise your heart rate <u>higher</u>.
The level of intensity at which training improves physical fitness is called the <u>training threshold</u>.

For more about training zones and target heart rates, see page 38.

T = TIME of activity — how <u>long</u> you should exercise.
<u>Aerobic</u> training sessions tend to last for <u>20 minutes</u> or <u>longer</u>.
<u>Strength</u> training sessions are generally <u>shorter</u> and <u>less sustained</u>.
A strength session might consist of <u>short sets</u> of sprints or weights, with <u>long rest periods</u> in between.

T = TYPE of activity — <u>what exercises</u> you should use.
It can be good to <u>vary</u> training sessions to <u>stop you tiring</u> of the same old workout. When applied to aerobic training this is called <u>cross training</u> — a different exercise (e.g. cycling instead of running) is used to <u>increase fitness</u>, but without <u>over-stressing</u> the tissues and joints used in the <u>main sport</u>. For example, rowers often supplement their training with some jogging and weights.

<u>Climatic conditions</u> can also affect the type of exercise — e.g. they can make training for some sports difficult in <u>winter</u>. One solution is to <u>travel abroad</u> for warm weather or altitude training — but of course this depends on having the necessary <u>funds</u> or <u>sponsorship</u>.

Get FITT (into your head) — it'll help in the exam...

Use FITT to get fit — Frequency, Intensity, Time and Type. Remember that the training has got to be suited to the individual — it's no good making an unfit businessman run 10 miles a day in his first week of training. And make sure that the training's not too boring, or you'll never do any...

Warm-Up and Worked Exam Questions

Warm-up Questions

1) What must you do after every training session?
2) What do the initials SPOR stand for?
3) What can you do to ensure you don't get bored when training?
4) What are the four stages of training for competition?
5) How often and for how long should a person exercise if they wish to stay healthy?
6) What is cross training?

Worked Exam Questions

Work through these exam questions carefully, making sure you understand them, then try the practice questions on the next page.

1   James is an elite performer. At the beginning of each training session he spends 10 minutes warming up.

a)   What are the benefits of a warm-up?

It focuses the mind and increases body temperature and blood flow to the muscles. It stretches the muscles, helping to increase the range of movement.

Check the number of marks before answering a question — it's a good guide to how much detail you need to go into.

(3 marks)

b)   Give an example of what could happen to James if he doesn't warm up.

He could injure himself / tear a muscle.

(1 mark)

2   April is designing a training programme for her GCSE coursework.

a)   What do the initials FITT stand for?

Frequency, Intensity, Time and Type.

(1 mark)

b)   Explain why you would need to use knowledge of FITT when designing a training programme.

To improve and get fitter you need to increase the frequency, intensity and time that you train for in order to keep pushing the body beyond the training threshold. You also need to change the type of activity, so that you don't overstress the tissues and joints used in the main sport, and to help prevent boredom.

Make sure you cover all four of the FITT principles in your answer.   *(4 marks)*

Exam Questions

1   Lisa has been unable to train for four weeks due to a groin strain.

    a)   What is likely to have happened to her fitness level?

    ....

    (1 mark)

    b)   What principle of training does this illustrate?

    ....

    (1 mark)

    c)   Describe the other three principles of training.

    ....

    ....

    ....

    (3 marks)

2   Janice is training for the London Marathon. Every other day she runs 10 miles, followed by a 15 minute walk to cool down. She is getting bored with the training and doesn't feel that she is improving.

    a)   How could Janice improve her training programme?

    ....

    ....

    ....

    (2 marks)

    b)   What are the benefits of a cool-down?

    ....

    ....

    (2 marks)

3   Philip is trying to organise his athletics training schedule for the year. Suggest how he can divide his year up to make this easier.

    ....

    ....

    ....

    ....

    ....

    (4 marks)

Training Methods

There's more to weight training than just pumping iron — you've got to <u>grunt</u> as well...
Oh yes and there are all these different ways of increasing strength too — with rather silly names...

Weight Training improves **Muscle Strength and Tone**

There are three kinds of strength: *See also page 41.*

1 Explosive strength — e.g. discus, shot-put.

2 Static strength — e.g. holding up a heavy weight.

3 Dynamic strength — e.g. moving a heavy object.

<u>OVERLOAD</u> is achieved by lifting the weights <u>more times</u>, or using <u>heavier weights</u>.

There are <u>two kinds</u> of weight training you need to know about: <u>Isometric</u> and <u>isotonic</u> training.

Isometric Training — Muscles **Contract**, but there's **No Movement**

ADVANTAGES

1) Develops <u>strength</u> — especially <u>static</u> strength.

2) <u>Cheap</u>, <u>quick</u> and easy to do <u>anywhere</u>.

DISADVANTAGES

1) Muscles gain most strength at the <u>angle</u> used in the isometric exercise — not necessarily the angle you use for your sport.

2) Not good if you've got <u>heart problems</u> — blood flow to the muscle is reduced during exercise, so the <u>blood pressure rises</u>, putting more strain on the heart for <u>little improvement in fitness</u>.

EXAMPLE: <u>The Wall Sit</u>
Sit with your back to the wall and your knees bent at 90° and hold it.

Isotonic Training —
Muscles **Contract** and **Shorten** producing **Movement**

ADVANTAGES

1) Strengthens the muscle throughout the <u>range of movement</u>.

2) Easily <u>adaptable</u> to suit most sports.

DISADVANTAGES

1) Muscles can become <u>sore</u> because of the <u>stress</u> they're under when <u>lengthening</u>.

2) Muscles gain the most strength when they're at their <u>weakest point</u> of action.

EXAMPLE: <u>Pull-ups</u>
Hang from a bar and then pull yourself up until your head is over it.

Weight training uses sets and repetitions:
A <u>repetition</u> is moving the weight once.
A <u>set</u> is the number of repetitions you do in one go.
For example, if you do <u>2 sets</u> of bar curls, with <u>15 repetitions</u> in each set, then you've lifted the weight <u>30 times</u>.

Learn this now — and take a weight off your mind...

Make sure you know the differences between the two types of weight training. One involves movement, and one doesn't. There's a little bit more about them on page 11.

Training Methods

And here are some more training methods. Make sure you learn them all...

Pressure Training Simulates the **Pressure of Competition**

The idea here is to increase the <u>pressure</u> on the player when training.
Ways to increase the pressure include:

1) '<u>One shot</u>' — in which only a single shot or attempt is allowed.

2) Using <u>visualisation</u> to imagine that you're in an important competition.

3) <u>Scoring methods</u> — scores are given to practice performances, and either the performances or the players in a team are <u>ranked</u>.

ADVANTAGES

1) Pressure training means you're more likely to <u>cope</u> with the <u>pressure</u> of a real competition.

2) It's especially useful for <u>high-pressure games</u> — e.g. tennis, or team sports like football.

DISADVANTAGES

1) The training can be <u>less enjoyable</u>.

2) It's not so much use to <u>amateurs</u>.

Circuit Training uses loads of **Different Exercises**

Each circuit has between 8 and 15 <u>stations</u> in it. At each station you do a <u>specific exercise</u> for a <u>set amount of time</u> before moving on to the next station. You're allowed a <u>short rest</u> between stations.

ADVANTAGES

1) <u>Less boring</u> because the exercises are all different.

2) <u>Easily adaptable</u> (can be done indoors and outdoors).

3) It can include <u>weight</u> training and <u>aerobic</u> exercise.

DISADVANTAGES

1) Can be a <u>pain to set up</u>.

2) People can <u>get in each other's way</u> if the circuit is busy.

<u>OVERLOAD</u> is achieved by doing <u>more repetitions</u> at each station, by completing the circuit more <u>quickly</u>, <u>resting less</u> between stations, or by <u>repeating</u> the circuit.

Pressure training — learn this page or you'll lose marks...

Another two important training methods to learn here. Make sure you know all the details. Circuit training can be adapted to any sport, so it's a really useful way to train...

Training Methods

So, you thought two pages would be enough to cover all the different training methods. Pah! Shows what you know. There's still <u>three more methods to learn</u>...

Continuous Training means **No Resting**

Continuous training involves exercising at a <u>constant rate</u> doing activities like <u>running</u> or <u>cycling</u>. It usually means exercising at <u>60-90%</u> of VO_2 Max for an <u>hour or more</u>. When done at the lower end of this VO_2 range, it is often referred to as <u>long, slow distance training</u> — or <u>LSD</u> for short.

ADVANTAGES

1) Needs only a <u>small amount</u> of easy-to-use <u>equipment</u>.
2) Good for <u>aerobic fitness</u> and using up <u>body fat</u>.

DISADVANTAGES

1) Can be really <u>boring</u>.
2) <u>Doesn't improve sprinting</u>, so not ideal for many <u>games</u>, like football and hockey.

<u>OVERLOAD</u> is achieved by increasing the <u>duration</u>, <u>distance</u>, <u>speed</u>, or <u>frequency</u> of training.

Fartlek Training is all about **Changes of Speed**

<u>Fartlek training</u> involves <u>changes in intensity</u> and <u>type</u> of exercise <u>without stopping</u>. For example, part of a fartlek run could be to <u>sprint</u> for 10 seconds, then <u>jog</u> for 20 seconds (repeated for 4 minutes) — followed by <u>long-stride running</u> for 2 minutes. It can be made easy or hard to <u>suit</u> your fitness and can be adapted to fit any <u>continuous exercise</u> (e.g. running, cycling, swimming, rowing).

ADVANTAGES

1) Good for sports that need <u>different paces</u>, like football and basketball.
2) Easily changed to <u>suit</u> an individual or a particular sport.

DISADVANTAGES

1) Difficult to see how <u>hard</u> the person is training.
2) Too easy to <u>skip the hard bits</u> if you can't be bothered.

<u>OVERLOAD</u> is achieved by increasing the <u>times</u> or <u>speeds</u> of each bit, or the <u>terrain</u> difficulty (e.g. running uphill).

Interval Training uses **Fixed Patterns of Exercise**

Fixed <u>patterns</u> of <u>fast and slow</u> exercise are used in interval training. Each repetition of a pattern is called a '<u>rep</u>' (repetition), and you've got to finish a '<u>set</u>' (group of reps) before a rest.

ADVANTAGES

1) Can mix aerobic and anaerobic exercise.
2) Easy to see when an athlete isn't trying.

DISADVANTAGES

1) Hard to keep going.
2) A bit dull.

<u>OVERLOAD</u> is achieved by increasing the <u>reps</u> or <u>sets</u>. Or by spending <u>less time resting</u> between sets.

Interval learning — revision, questions, revision, questions, revision...
This section on training methods doesn't mess around — everything does exactly what it says in the heading, except fartlek training, which actually means 'speed play' in Swedish. How nice...

Warm-Up and Worked Exam Questions

Warm-up Questions

1) Which one of the following is an example of explosive strength — being a member of the pack in a rugby scrum, a sprinter leaving the starting blocks or doing a set of press-ups?
2) Which type of weight training develops static strength — isometric or isotonic?
3) In isometric training, do the muscles contract to produce movement?
4) Describe fartlek training.
5) Give one disadvantage of continuous training.
6) Name one type of training that can be used for improving both aerobic and anaerobic fitness?

Worked Exam Questions

Go through these questions, and then have a go at the ones on the opposite page on your own.
The more practice you do, the easier it gets...

1   There are two different types of weight training. One of them is isometric training.

a)   Name the other type of weight training.

Isotonic

(1 mark)

b)   Explain the difference between the two types of weight training, providing examples of each.

In isometric training, the muscles contract but there is no

movement, e.g. doing a wall sit. In isotonic training the muscles

contract and shorten to produce movement, e.g. doing pull-ups.

Remember to give examples when the question asks for them
— in this question, the examples are worth half the marks.

(4 marks)

c)   Give two disadvantages of isometric training

Raises blood pressure, putting extra strain on the heart. Muscles

gain most strength at the angle used in the exercise.

(2 marks)

2   Sharon wants to improve her endurance by using fartlek training, but she has been told that it can be difficult to see how hard you are training using this method.

a)   Name two other types of training she could do.

Circuit training or continuous training.

You could also put interval training here.

(2 marks)

b)   Give two advantages of fartlek training.

It's good training for sports that need different speeds and it can be

easily changed to suit the individual.

Make sure you know the advantages and the disadvantages for all types of training.   *(2 marks)*

Exam Questions

1   George is training for the school cross-country team.

   a)   Which type of endurance training would be the most suitable for this, and why?

   ....

   ....

   (2 marks)

   b)   Give one disadvantage of this type of training.

   ....

   (1 mark)

   c)   How could George make his training sessions harder?

   ....

   ....

   (2 marks)

2   Shaun is training for his next tennis match. He wants to practise under match conditions.
     His coach is scoring each practice performance.

   a)   What type of training is Shaun doing?

   ....

   (1 mark)

   b)   Name two disadvantages of this type of training.

   ....

   ....

   (2 marks)

3   Fiona is a hockey player. Her friend Vicky runs cross-country. They want to train
     together to encourage each other.

   a)   Suggest a type of endurance training that would suit both sports.

   ....

   (1 mark)

   b)   Vicky has decided to do an extra continuous training session once a week.
        How long and how hard should she work?

   ....

   ....

   (2 marks)

   c)   Which aspect of Fiona's performance may this type of training not develop?

   ....

   (1 mark)

Aerobic Fitness Testing

You've got to know what <u>aerobic fitness</u> is, how to <u>measure</u> it and how to <u>improve</u> it.

It's Good to have a **High Aerobic Fitness Level**

If you've got a <u>high aerobic fitness level</u>, it should mean that compared with people of average fitness:

1) Your <u>heart rate</u> will be <u>lower</u> when resting, and when exercising.

2) You can <u>exercise for longer</u> without feeling tired.

3) You can use up <u>more oxygen</u> when you're exercising.

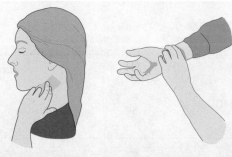

CAROTID ARTERY   RADIAL ARTERY

MEASURING YOUR HEART RATE

Put your first two fingers on one of these <u>two pulse points</u>:

1) **CAROTID ARTERY** — on your <u>neck</u>, to the side of the lumpy bit in the middle.

2) **RADIAL ARTERY** — that's on your <u>wrist</u>, by the base of your thumb.

Count the beats over <u>fifteen seconds</u> (e.g. 17). Multiply that number by <u>four</u> ($17 \times 4 = 68$) to get your <u>beats per minute</u> — that's your <u>heart rate</u> (heart rate is 68 beats per minute).

There are **Three Main Tests** for Aerobic Fitness

HARVARD STEP TEST

1) Using a <u>45 cm step</u>, do <u>30 step-ups a minute</u> for <u>5 minutes</u>. (Or if you have to go slower, keep going for 20 seconds after you begin to slow down, then stop.)

2) <u>Rest for 1 minute</u>, then take your <u>pulse</u> for 15 seconds — multiply this by 4 to get your heart rate.

3) Use this formula to work out your <u>score</u>. The <u>higher</u> your score, the <u>fitter</u> you are.

$$\frac{\text{length of exercise in seconds} \times 100}{5.5 \times \text{pulse count}}$$

4) There are different <u>versions</u> of the Harvard step test, so check the details (height of the step, rest time etc.) before comparing results.

12-MINUTE RUN

1) <u>Jog</u> to warm up.

2) When a whistle sounds, <u>run</u> round a track <u>as many times as you can</u> in <u>12 minutes</u>.

3) The distance you run is recorded. The <u>further</u> you can run, the <u>fitter</u> you are.

MULTISTAGE FITNESS TEST

1) You must run 'shuttles' between <u>2 lines</u>, 20 metres apart. Start on the first <u>bleep</u>.

2) Your foot must be <u>on or over</u> the next line when the next bleep sounds.

3) The time between bleeps gets <u>shorter</u>, so you have to run <u>faster</u>.

4) If you <u>miss a beep</u> you are allowed <u>two</u> further beeps to <u>catch up</u>. If you miss <u>three</u> beeps in a row, the level and number of shuttles completed are noted as your <u>final score</u>.

5) Your <u>Maximal Oxygen Consumption</u> (VO_2 max) can then be calculated.

6) The <u>higher</u> your Maximal Oxygen Consumption, the <u>fitter</u> you are.

See page 15 for more about VO_2 max.

Three different tests to learn — and they're all really nasty...

There's no way to test your aerobic fitness without making you really, really tired. My advice is to learn the theory, and then try to avoid trying it out on yourself. And make sure you learn how to take your pulse.

Fitness Testing

Aerobic fitness isn't the only thing you'll need to know how to test. You've also got to know about testing <u>muscular endurance</u>, <u>strength</u> and <u>flexibility</u>. Here's the info — get learning.

There are Different **Tests** for Different **Types** of Fitness

Fitness <u>isn't just</u> how long you can <u>run</u> for or how much you can <u>lift</u>. Overall fitness includes endurance, strength, power, agility and flexibility — you can <u>measure</u> each with a different test.

MUSCULAR ENDURANCE TESTING
Test the endurance of different muscles by seeing <u>how many times</u> you can do an <u>exercise</u> — e.g. the sit-up test measures the number of sit-ups you can do in 30 seconds.

BALANCE TESTING — THE STORK STAND TEST
Stand on your best leg with your other foot touching your knee, <u>eyes closed</u> and your hands on your hips. Time how long you can stand there. Wobbling's allowed, but <u>no moving your feet or hands</u>, or <u>opening your eyes</u>. Take the <u>best of three</u> times.

SPEED TESTING
Any test that involves moving <u>fast over a short distance</u> will be good for this. E.g. the sprint test — simply time how long it takes you to run 100m.

By <u>repeating</u> these tests (e.g. every few weeks), you can see if your performance has <u>improved</u>.

STRENGTH TESTING
This kind of <u>dynamometer</u> measures <u>hand</u> and <u>forearm</u> strength. Just grip as hard as you can...

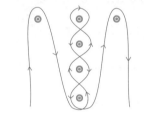

Any test <u>longer than 30 seconds</u> isn't a good strength test — it's better for testing <u>muscular endurance</u>.

AGILITY TESTING
Test agility by setting up any kind of <u>course</u> that means <u>changing direction</u> frequently and timing the run.

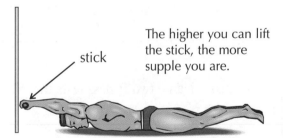

This is a typical agility run.

You Have to Stretch to Test **Flexibility**

There are loads of <u>different ways</u> to test flexibility — but most of them just measure <u>how far you can stretch</u>. You do different stretches to measure <u>different parts</u> of the body.

SHOULDER LIFT TEST
This measures flexibility at the <u>shoulders</u>.
1) Lie <u>face down</u> on the floor.
2) Grab a 50 cm <u>stick</u> with both hands, keeping your hands <u>shoulder width apart</u>.
3) <u>Raise</u> the stick with <u>straight arms</u> — but keep your <u>chin on the floor</u>.
4) Measure <u>how far</u> you can raise the stick off the floor.

stick

The higher you can lift the stick, the more supple you are.

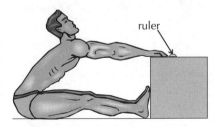
ruler

SIT AND REACH TEST
This measures flexibility in the <u>back</u> and <u>hamstrings</u>.
1) <u>Sit</u> on the floor with your legs pointing straight out in front of you.
2) Push a <u>ruler</u>, placed on a box, <u>as far forwards</u> as you can with your fingers — keeping your <u>legs straight</u> all the time.

Learn this page — and give your brain a stretch...
Just like you get tested on how much you know about PE, athletes get tested on things like muscle strength, endurance and their flexibility — so you've got to know how to test them. There's not that much you can learn about a dynamometer, but make sure you know the sit and reach test really well.

Warm-Up and Exam Questions

1) What equipment do you need to measure strength?
2) Where on the body can you take your pulse?
3) Name a test for balance.
4) What does VO$_2$ max mean?

Exam Questions

It's time to test what's covered over the last two pages. There's no worked exam questions this time because this is such a short section. And let's face it — you're so great at PE, you don't need the extra help.

1   Charlene is a good club-level gymnast. She prefers to work on the beam.

a)   Name two types of fitness that she needs to work on the beam.

....

(2 marks)

b)   For one of these types of fitness, suggest a suitable test she could use to measure it and describe the procedure for carrying out this test.

....

....

....

(3 marks)

2   Shaun believes that he has a high aerobic fitness level.

a)   If Shaun does have a high aerobic fitness level, how will he differ from people of average aerobic fitness?

....

....

(3 marks)

b)   Name two fitness tests that Shaun could use to see if he is right.

....

....

(2 marks)

c)   Describe the procedure for one of these tests.

....

....

....

....

(2 marks)

Sporting Injuries

There are two different types of injury that you can get from playing sport — <u>chronic</u> and <u>acute</u> injuries.

Chronic Injuries are Caused by *Overuse*

CHRONIC INJURIES — caused by <u>continuous stress</u> on part of the body over a <u>long period</u> of time:

1) Tennis players can develop <u>tennis elbow</u> — a painful inflammation of tendons in the elbow due to overuse of certain arm muscles.

2) Golfers get a similar chronic injury called, wait for it... <u>golfer's elbow</u>.

3) <u>Long-distance runners</u> can develop a nasty bone injury in the leg called <u>shin splints</u>.

4) You're at risk of a chronic injury if you <u>train too hard</u>, <u>don't rest enough</u> between training sessions, use <u>poor footwear</u>, or have <u>bad technique</u>.

Acute Injuries are Caused by a *Sudden Stress*

ACUTE INJURIES — happen when there's a <u>sudden stress</u> on the body. They come in all sorts of nasty forms, like <u>bone fractures</u>, <u>pulled muscles</u>, and <u>concussion</u> — and they're caused by things like:

1) <u>Colliding</u> with an opponent or obstacle, e.g. in sports like rugby and football.

2) <u>Being hit</u> by something, e.g. a cricket ball, squash racket or boxing glove.

3) <u>Falling</u>
   a) from a <u>height</u>, e.g. in rock-climbing, mountaineering or skiing.
   b) at high <u>speed</u>, e.g. in skiing, cycling, horse racing or running.

A Lot of Injuries *can be Prevented*

BEFORE SPORT

1) Take off anything that could get <u>caught</u> (e.g. jewellery, watches).

2) Use the right <u>equipment</u> — and check it's in <u>good condition</u>.

3) Watch out for possible dangers in the <u>playing environment</u>, e.g. stones or glass hidden in grass, or slippery patches caused by bad weather.

4) Make sure the <u>weather</u> is not a danger — this is especially important for <u>outdoor adventure activities</u> like hillwalking, sailing and climbing.

5) Use the correct <u>technique</u>, including when <u>lifting/carrying/placing equipment</u>.

6) <u>Warm up</u> before the activity, making sure you exercise the <u>muscles you're going to use</u>.

DURING SPORT

1) Play with people of a <u>similar size</u>, <u>strength</u> and <u>skill level</u> — this is known as '<u>balancing</u>' a competition.

2) Know and follow the <u>rules</u> of the game.

3) Use the <u>correct technique</u>.

4) Wear <u>appropriate clothing</u> (e.g. clothing may get caught if it is too loose), and <u>suitable footwear</u> (e.g. studded football boots, spiked running shoes). Good sports shoes should support the <u>arches</u> of your feet, and <u>cushion the ankle joint</u> from impacts.

5) Use <u>protective clothing/equipment</u> where appropriate (e.g. padding in cricket, cycling helmet).

6) Use <u>officials</u> (e.g. a referee) to ensure there's <u>fair play</u> and to make sure that the <u>rules</u> are <u>followed</u>. If you're using a swimming pool, make sure there's a qualified <u>lifeguard</u>.

AFTERWARDS

1) <u>Cool down</u> properly.

2) Give yourself plenty of time to <u>recover</u> before playing again.

Remember — prevention is better than cure...

For both chronic and acute injuries, think of places and events where they're most likely to happen.

Sporting Injuries

Injuries are also categorised as soft-tissue or hard-tissue injuries. It's simple enough — hard-tissue injuries are when the bone is damaged, and soft-tissue injuries are all the others.

Most Sporting Injuries are to Soft Tissue

OPEN INJURIES
Open injuries are where the skin's broken, usually letting blood escape. They're things like cuts, grazes, blisters and chafing.

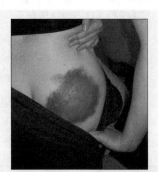

CLOSED INJURIES
Closed injuries happen beneath the skin — there's no external bleeding.

1) Bruising is when your blood vessels get damaged — you bleed inside.

2) Strained (pulled) muscles and tendons have tears in the tissue — they're caused by sudden overstretching. Pulled hamstrings and calf muscles are common injuries in loads of sports like football and cricket.

Bruising can look spectacular — but it's usually not that serious.

3) Sprains are joint injuries where the ligament has been stretched or torn, usually because of violent twisting.

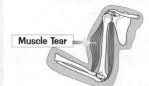

Muscle Tear

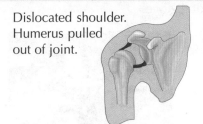
Dislocated shoulder. Humerus pulled out of joint.

4) Joints can get dislocated as well. The bone is pulled out of its normal position — again, it's twisting that usually does it.

5) Cartilage can also be damaged. E.g. the cartilage of the knee can be torn by a violent impact or twisting motion. This injury is common in sports like football.

Hard-Tissue Injuries are Bone Fractures

Fractures are either cracks in the bone or an actual break. All hard-tissue injuries are bone fractures. Just like with soft-tissue injuries, they can be open or closed.

1) Fractures are usually accompanied by bruising and swelling. This is because they damage blood vessels in or around the bone.

2) They'll also cause a lot of pain because of the damaged nerves inside the bone.

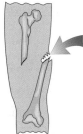

In an **open fracture** the skin is torn and the bone pokes out. Urgghh.

In a **closed fracture** it all happens under the skin. The skin itself is alright.

STRESS FRACTURES
A 'stress fracture' is a crack along the length of a bone. It's caused by continuous stress over a long period of time (so it's a chronic injury). All other bone fractures are acute injuries. Long-distance runners get stress fractures called shin splints.

Open fractures are also called compound fractures...

If the skin's broken it's an open injury, otherwise it's closed — that's easy enough to remember. Make sure you can recall every injury mentioned here, describe what it is, and give examples of where it happens. And remember, sprains are a bit like strains but they happen at the joints.

Injury — Types and Treatment

And here's some more lovely stuff on <u>injuries</u> and <u>treating</u> them. Enjoy...

The **RICE Method** treats **Minor Soft-Tissue** Injuries

The <u>RICE method</u> is a good treatment for <u>soft-tissue injuries</u> like sprains, strains or bruises.
It <u>reduces pain</u>, <u>swelling</u> and <u>bruising</u>. But don't use it if you think there may be a <u>fracture</u>.

It's sometimes just known as <u>ICE</u> (well, the 'R' bit is pretty obvious).

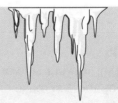

R — REST	<u>Stop immediately</u> and <u>rest</u> the injury — if you carry on, you'll make it worse.
I — ICE	<u>Apply ice</u> to the injury. This makes the blood vessels <u>contract</u> to reduce internal <u>bleeding</u> and <u>swelling</u>.
C — COMPRESSION	<u>Bandaging</u> the injury will also help <u>reduce swelling</u>. But don't make it so <u>tight</u> that you stop the blood circulating altogether.
E — ELEVATION	Support the limb at a <u>raised level</u> (i.e. above the heart). This <u>reduces</u> the flow of blood because it has to flow against gravity.

Severe Environments can cause Serious Conditions

HYPERTHERMIA

SYMPTOMS
Body temperature gets too high — weak pulse, clammy pale skin.
Results from over-exercising and dehydration (lack of water), especially on a hot day.
Long-distance runners and cyclists are particularly at risk.

TREATMENT
Lay the patient down in a cool place, and give them liquids.
Get advice from a doctor.

HYPOTHERMIA

SYMPTOMS
Body temperature falls below 35 °C. Muscles go rigid,
heart beats irregularly, casualty may fall unconscious.

TREATMENT
Steadily raise body temperature to 37 °C. Put them into warm, dry clothing or wrap
them in a blanket. Give them hot drinks, and maybe a warm (but not hot) bath.

Who ever thought that RICE could be so useful?

The RICE method is really important — you've got to know when to use it and when not to use it —
don't if there might be a fracture. You don't want to go monkeying around with a broken leg unless you
know what you're doing. And don't get your hyperthermia confused with your hypothermia either...

Injury — Types and Treatment

Here are some more assorted ailments that you need to know about.
Make sure you know them all, and how to <u>treat</u> them.

Cramp, *Concussion*, *Stitch* — other Common Problems

Cramp

SYMPTOMS

<u>Involuntary contraction</u> of a muscle caused by <u>lack of salt</u> minerals in the blood, or by <u>lack of blood</u> flowing to a muscle. It's painful, but easy to treat.

TREATMENT

Just <u>stretch</u> the muscle and hold it like that, <u>massaging</u> it gently, until the muscle relaxes.

Winding

SYMPTOMS

<u>Difficulty in breathing</u>, <u>pain</u> in the abdomen, and might feel <u>sick</u>. Caused by a <u>blow to the abdomen</u>.

TREATMENT

<u>Stop</u> exercising, <u>lean forward</u>, and <u>rub</u> the affected area.

Shock

SYMPTOMS

Pale, clammy skin. Rapid, weak <u>pulse</u> and <u>breathing</u>.
May feel weak, faint, sick, dizzy or thirsty. Caused by a drop in <u>blood pressure</u>.

TREATMENT

Call an <u>ambulance</u>, stem any external <u>bleeding</u>, <u>reassure</u> them, place in <u>recovery position</u>.

Concussion

SYMPTOMS

Unconsciousness, disorientation, memory loss. Caused by a <u>blow to the head</u>.

TREATMENT

If unconscious, place in the <u>recovery position</u> (see page 75) and get an ambulance.
If conscious, keep casualty under <u>observation</u> for 24 hours.

Stitch

SYMPTOMS

A sharp <u>pain</u> in your side or abdomen. It's basically <u>cramp of the diaphragm</u> and can make <u>breathing</u> difficult. Caused by vigorous exercise too soon after <u>eating</u>.

TREATMENT

Stop exercising, take deep breaths, and breathe out slowly.

Disorientation and memory loss — the symptoms of exam panic...

Well, it goes without saying that you need to learn everything on this page. *(and concussion)*
For each condition or injury, practise scribbling down the symptoms and the treatments until you're getting them all right. There's nothing complicated here — just some old-fashioned learning...

Injury — Types and Treatment

The <u>DRABC</u> first-aid treatment is for <u>serious injuries</u> where the casualty seems to be <u>unconscious</u>. DRABC stands for Danger, Response, Airway, Breathing, Circulation — the things to check first.

Use **DRABC** if they seem to be **Unconscious**

D — CHECK FOR ANY IMMEDIATE DANGER

1) Make sure there's no <u>danger</u> to you or the casualty.
2) <u>Clear</u> the surrounding area, and <u>stop any games</u>.

R — CHECK FOR A RESPONSE

1) Check if they're <u>conscious</u>. Ask if they can hear you. If not, gently shake them to see if they respond.
2) If they're unconscious, continue with <u>ABC</u>.

A — MAKE SURE THE AIRWAY IS CLEAR

1) <u>Tilt</u> the head back.
2) Check the tongue's not <u>blocking</u> the airway.
3) <u>Loosen</u> tight clothing. Clear away any vomit.

B — LOOK FOR SIGNS OF BREATHING

1) Look at their <u>chest</u> to see if it's moving.
2) Put your cheek by their mouth — try to feel their <u>breath</u>.

C — CHECK FOR CIRCULATION

Feel the <u>neck</u> to see if the casualty has a pulse (carotid pulse).

IF THE CASUALTY IS BREATHING ➤ PUT CASUALTY INTO THE RECOVERY POSITION.

IF THERE'S A PULSE BUT NO BREATHING ➤ GIVE MOUTH-TO-MOUTH VENTILATION UNTIL BREATHING RETURNS.

IF THERE'S NO PULSE ➤ GIVE MOUTH-TO-MOUTH VENTILATION WITH CARDIAC MASSAGE TO KEEP BLOOD FLOWING.

Mouth-to-mouth and <u>cardiac massage</u> are covered on the next page.

An <u>ambulance</u> should be called at the <u>earliest opportunity</u>.

Easy as DR-ABC...

The ABC bit is the actual first aid, but you need to do the whole DRABC thing if you're the first to arrive at the scene. But remember you still need to get an ambulance as soon as you possibly can. Checking for danger is an easy one to forget in the exam, but it's really important.

Injury — Types and Treatment

The last page told you what <u>order</u> you should do things in if you have to treat an unconscious person. Here's the <u>procedures</u> you might need to use to keep them alive.

Mouth-to-mouth *keeps the casualty supplied with* oxygen

The idea of mouth-to-mouth ventilation is for you to <u>breathe for the casualty</u>, forcing oxygen from your lungs into theirs. Here's how you do it:

1 <u>Tilt</u> the casualty's head back, <u>open</u> their mouth and <u>pinch</u> their nose closed.

2 <u>Breathe in</u> deeply, then press your lips onto theirs and <u>breathe out</u> slowly, making sure their <u>chest rises</u>.

3 Take your mouth <u>away</u> and let their chest <u>fall</u> again.

<u>Repeat</u> these steps until breathing returns or help arrives.

Cardiac massage *keeps the* blood circulating

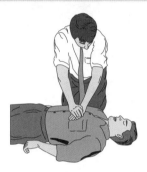

If a casualty has <u>no pulse</u>, cardiac massage can be used to keep blood <u>circulating</u> around their body. Here's how:

1 Do <u>2 breaths</u> of mouth-to-mouth ventilation.

2 <u>Press down</u> on the <u>chest 15 times</u>, a bit faster than once a second.

3 <u>Repeat</u> this pattern — 2 breaths, 15 chest compressions.

4 Look for <u>signs of improvement</u>, e.g. skin colour returning. Check for a pulse every minute.

DON'T TRY CARDIAC MASSAGE UNLESS YOU'VE HAD PROPER TRAINING. Doing cardiac massage in the wrong way, or in the wrong circumstances could make matters worse.

DON'T PRACTISE THIS ON SOMEONE WHO'S CONSCIOUS.

Mouth-to-mouth and cardiac massage <u>together</u> are called <u>cardiopulmonary resuscitation</u> (or <u>CPR</u>).

Finally, place in the Recovery Position

Once they're <u>breathing okay</u>, you can put the casualty into the <u>recovery position</u>.

In this position, the head is <u>tilted</u> so that the airway won't be <u>blocked</u> by the tongue or by vomit. You should be able to <u>leave</u> the person unconscious like this while you go for <u>help</u>.

Learn this — it could save someone's life...

Remember — mouth-to-mouth is to restore breathing, cardiac massage is to keep blood flowing. But don't go trying them out willy-nilly. This page only gives you the theory — it's not proper practical first-aid training. I remember the episode of ER when someone did CPR on a casualty with broken ribs...

Warm-Up and Worked Exam Questions

Warm-up Questions

1) What is meant by 'balancing' a competition?
2) What is the difference between a soft-tissue injury and a hard-tissue injury?
3) What does RICE stand for?
4) What would you do if a casualty had a pulse but was not breathing?
5) Name an injury caused by overuse.
6) What is the difference between an open and a closed injury?

Worked Exam Questions

Here's some preventative treatment — go through these worked exam questions carefully, then try the exam questions on the next page. That should reduce the risk of a nasty accident come the exam.

1   Many sports performers suffer from injuries during their careers.

    a)   What are the two categories of tissue injuries that can happen?

Soft-tissue injuries and hard-tissue injuries.

(2 marks)

    b)   Explain the difference between a sprain and a strain.

A sprain is a joint injury where a ligament is stretched or torn.

A strain is a tear in a muscle or tendon.

(2 marks)

    c)   Explain how you would treat a strain.

Rest the injury, apply ice to it, apply compression using a bandage

and elevate the injured body part so that it is higher than the heart.

          Don't just say RICE — say what you would actually do.   *(2 marks)*

2   Tim trains seven days a week. He gives himself little time to recover between sessions.

    a)   What type of injury may he suffer from if he continues to do this?

He could get an overuse injury / chronic injury

(1 mark)

    b)   There are several things that an athlete can do to prevent injuries from happening. Identify two things that can be done during a game to reduce the risks.

Players should know and follow the rules of the game and wear

appropriate clothing.

          There are other possible answers for both of these questions.   *(2 marks)*

    c)   Name two things that could be done before a game to reduce the risks.

Players should take off anything that could get caught on things,

and warm up properly.

(2 marks)

Exam Questions

1   Rosie is completing her Duke of Edinburgh Award. She camped out with her group overnight in freezing conditions.

    a)   What condition are they at risk from? What are the symptoms?

    ....

    ....

    ....

(3 marks)

    b)   How could Rosie treat someone in the group who was suffering from this condition?

    ....

    ....

(3 marks)

    If the weather had been hot during their expedition they may also have been at risk.

    c)   What condition might this have caused? What are the symptoms and how would you treat the condition?

    ....

    ....

    ....

(3 marks)

2   George has fallen off his trail bike and his leg is painful. There is a lot of swelling.

    a)   George thinks he might have damaged the bone. What type of injury is this?

    ....

(1 mark)

    b)   There are two main types of break that your bones can have.
    Name these and explain the difference between them.

    ....

    ....

    ....

    ....

(4 marks)

    c)   Is this an example of an acute or a chronic injury? Explain your answer.

    ....

(1 mark)

Exam Questions

3   Many professional football players plant their studs in the ground and try to turn as they kick the ball.

a)   What types of injury could this cause?

....

(1 mark)

At half time, one of the players on a football team lies on his back and has his leg stretched by the team physiotherapist.

b)   What could the player be suffering from, and what causes this condition?

....

....

....

(3 marks)

c)   What does cardiopulmonary resuscitation (CPR) involve?

....

....

(2 marks)

4   Michelle's friend has been hit on the head by a hockey ball and seems to be unconscious.

a)   Describe the first-aid treatment that Michelle should use.

....

....

....

....

(3 marks)

Michelle's friend comes round, but feels dizzy and looks very pale.

b)   What may be wrong with her?

....

(1 mark)

c)   What is the correct treatment?

....

(1 mark)

Skills

Skill is a word we use all the time. In PE, it's got a very fancy definition which you need to learn:

> **A SKILL IS A LEARNED ABILITY TO BRING ABOUT THE RESULT YOU WANT, WITH MAXIMUM CERTAINTY AND EFFICIENCY.**

1) So the main point is that a skill is something you've got to learn. You can't be born with a skill, although you might learn it faster than other people.

2) With any skill, you always have a result in mind — you know what you want to do.

3) Skills should be performed with control and the minimum expense of energy/time.

Skills can be **Basic** or **Complex**

We say that particular actions which agree with the points above are skills, e.g. throwing a dart.

Running is a basic skill

BASIC SKILLS — simple things like jumping or throwing:

1) You tend to master a lot of basic skills at an early age.

2) Basic skills tend to be transferable between many different activities. Just think of all the sports where you need a basic skill like running.

3) When learning a new sport or activity, it's really important that you've mastered all the basic skills first, before you attempt the more complex ones.

COMPLEX SKILLS — need a higher level of coordination and control:

1) Most complex skills are specific to one particular sport — like taking a football penalty kick (i.e. they're usually non-transferable).

2) They take more practice to master and have more scope for improvement — e.g. in tennis you'd spend more time improving your forehand than practising a basic skill like running.

Pole vaulting is a complex skill.

Skills are **Open**, **Closed** or Somewhere **In between**

1) Skills (as with so much in PE) can be open or closed.

2) An open skill is one which is affected by many external factors, e.g. in golf, you can't just go up to the ball and take a swing, oblivious to what's going on around you. You need to consider things like the position of the hole, obstacles like trees, and the effect of the wind.

3) A closed skill is one hardly affected by the environment or external factors, e.g. in darts, you usually make the same movements — you don't need to change them for different conditions.

4) To confuse the issue, most skills actually fall somewhere in between, e.g. taking a football penalty — your environment doesn't change much, but you can alter your movement to change the speed and aim of the shot in response to the positioning of the goalkeeper. So it's partly closed and partly open.

5) You can compare the "openness" of skills by putting them on a continuous scale like this one:

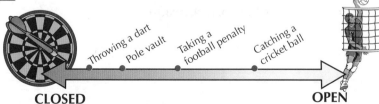

Throwing a dart   Pole vault   Taking a football penalty   Catching a cricket ball

CLOSED   OPEN

Revision — a closed skill...

Open skills can be affected by your opponents, as well as by the environment...

Skills

I know this page looks more like some <u>dull</u> IT module, but what it's actually about is the way your <u>brain works</u>, and how it <u>processes information</u> when you're learning a new skill.

The Brain *Processes Information*

This is the <u>basic model</u> of what your brain's up to when you're performing a <u>skill</u> (like when you're passing a football to someone else):

1 INPUT — this is all the <u>information</u> your brain <u>receives</u>. You <u>see</u> the position of the ball and the player you're aiming for. You <u>hear</u> players shouting. You <u>feel</u> the position of your feet and arms.

2 DECISION MAKING — this is where your brain <u>processes the information</u> and <u>decides</u> how to act.

3 OUTPUT — this is the actual <u>action</u> you carry out at the <u>end</u>, e.g. moving your leg to kick the ball.

4 FEEDBACK — the most <u>important</u> part of the learning process. Your brain looks at the <u>result</u> of the output and <u>registers</u> this information, so you'll <u>know better</u> next time. There are many ways of getting feedback:

1) You can <u>feel</u> how well you kicked the ball — <u>intrinsic feedback</u>.

2) You get <u>verbal feedback</u> from others, e.g. from a <u>coach</u> or teacher — <u>extrinsic feedback</u>.

3) You can <u>see how successful</u> the performance was. Did the ball go where it was aimed? Did the intended player get it?

Memory *and* Perception

1) When your brain gets all the <u>information</u> (input), it has to <u>interpret</u> what it all means. This is called <u>perception</u>.

2) It <u>filters out</u> all the junk — <u>selective attention</u>.

3) The brain <u>searches</u> really quickly through all its stuff about sport — <u>memories</u> of similar situations.

4) And by thinking about the <u>past outcomes</u> stored in the memory, the brain can make an <u>informed decision</u> of how best to <u>respond</u> — I suppose that's what learning from experience is all about.

Selective *Attention*

1) The brain has a <u>limited channel capacity</u> — i.e. it can only process a certain amount of information at a time.

2) It has to <u>filter out</u> all the extra information it receives and only process the information <u>relevant</u> to performing the skill.

3) This is called <u>selective attention</u>.

So here's an <u>extended version</u> of the basic diagram:

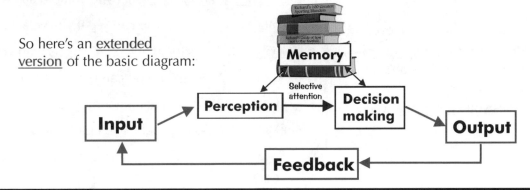

Information processing? Referee! — this isn't PE...

The flow diagrams are called information processing models. Practise drawing them...

Motivation and Mental Preparation

You've got to be physically fit to perform well at most sports — but it's <u>just as important</u> to be <u>mentally fit</u>. <u>Attitude</u> and <u>motivation</u> can really affect your performance. Here's how...

Motivation can be *Intrinsic* or *Extrinsic*

Motivation's about <u>how keen</u> you are to do something. It's what drives you on when things get difficult — your <u>desire to succeed</u>. You need to know about <u>two kinds</u>:

INTRINSIC MOTIVATION
This comes from <u>inside</u> you. You play the sport because it's something you <u>enjoy</u> and would <u>want to do well</u> at — even if there were no prizes or rewards.

EXTRINSIC MOTIVATION
This comes from <u>outside</u>. Maybe you want to do well because there's a big <u>reward</u> for succeeding — money or publicity, for example.

Your *Arousal Level* shouldn't be Too High

Arousal is about being <u>excited</u>, <u>keen</u> and <u>mentally ready</u> (or unready) to perform a difficult task.

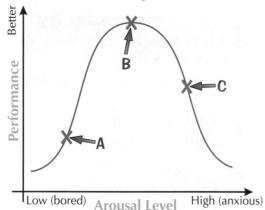

At **A**, the competitor <u>isn't very excited</u> — they're not very aroused — and so will probably <u>not</u> perform at their <u>best</u>.

At **B**, the competitor is <u>determined</u> and <u>ready</u> — their arousal level is <u>just right</u> — this should mean that they <u>perform well</u>.

At **C**, the competitor is <u>anxious</u> and <u>nervous</u> — their arousal level is too high. They may become '<u>psyched out</u>' or 'stressed out', and they <u>won't</u> be able to give their best performance.

This is the <u>Inverted U Theory of Arousal</u> (since the graph looks like an upside-down letter 'U'). <u>Too much</u> or <u>too little</u> arousal stops you performing at your best — the best level is in the <u>middle</u>.

Goal Setting should be *SMARTER*

Goal setting means setting <u>targets</u> that you want to reach. <u>Short-term</u> goals that you can reach quite quickly are <u>steps</u> on the way to a <u>long-term</u> one — like winning an Olympic medal.

GOAL SETTING
— helps training, because it:

1) Helps you <u>get ready to perform</u>, since you know what you want to achieve.

2) Helps you to <u>feel in control</u>, and so less anxious about a performance.

3) Gives you <u>confidence</u> when you reach a target.

4) <u>Motivates</u> you to work hard.

When you're setting goals, remember **SMARTER**.

S — <u>SPECIFIC</u>: Say <u>exactly</u> what you want to achieve.

M — <u>MEASURABLE</u>: So you can <u>see</u> if you've achieved it or not.

A — <u>AGREED</u>: You should <u>agree</u> the targets with your coach.

R — <u>REALISTIC</u>: Set goals you can <u>realistically</u> reach.

T — <u>TIME-PHASED</u>: So the long-term goal is reached <u>in time</u>.

E — <u>EXCITING</u>: Boring goals <u>won't</u> motivate you.

R — <u>RECORDED</u>: So that you can <u>check</u> your progress.

Psyched up — not psyched out...
Remember the name 'Inverted U Theory' — that'll impress the examiners, which is always good.

Warm-Up and Worked Exam Questions

Warm-up Questions

1) Give an example of a basic skill.
2) Which type of skill is affected by the environment — open or closed?
3) What are the two types of motivation? How do they differ?
4) What is selective attention?
5) What does SMARTER stand for?
6) What happens to you if your arousal level is too high?

Worked Exam Questions

You know the drill by now... study these worked exam questions making sure you fully understand them, then flip over the page to try some yourself.

1   Skills can be classified as being either open or closed.

    a)   How else can skills be classified?

Basic or complex
....

(1 mark)

    b)   Explain the difference between an open and a closed skill, providing examples of each.

An open skill is something that is affected by external factors,

e.g. catching a ball could be affected by the wind. A closed skill is

hardly affected by external factors, e.g. a forward roll.

        Don't forget those examples — they're worth half the marks.   *(4 marks)*

2   Katie is playing basketball for her school. She is receiving extrinsic feedback from her teacher.

    a)   Explain what extrinsic feedback is?

Advice / evaluation of performance from someone else.

For example, a coach telling you what is wrong with your technique.

        Use examples where it helps to explain the point.   *(2 marks)*

    Feedback is one part of the learning process. The brain receives it as "input".

    b)   Explain what input is, and give a sporting example.

Input is all the information your brain receives. For example, a

footballer can see their team-mates and the football. They can hear

the calls and feel where their arms and legs are.

        This is a three mark question, so you need to define "input" and then give at   *(3 marks)*
        least two types of input that someone playing your chosen sport might receive.

Exam Questions

1   Nancy plays netball regularly for her club. She has intrinsic motivation.

a)   What is intrinsic motivation?

....

(1 mark)

b)   What is the other type of motivation? How does it differ from intrinsic motivation?

....

....

....

(4 marks)

2   George, Peter and Dan are competing over 100 m. They all have different arousal
      levels. George is very relaxed, Peter is nervous and Dan is determined.

a)   Who is most likely to be able to perform at their best and why?

....

....

(2 marks)

b)   Fred, who also ran, used goal-setting to help him train. Give four ways in which
      goal-setting can help athletes perform at their best.

....

....

....

....

(4 marks)

3   Football players need several skills to be able to play well.

a)   Define the word "skill"?

....

....

(2 marks)

b)   Is taking a football penalty a closed skill or an open skill? Explain your answer.

....

....

....

(3 marks)

Revision Summary for Section Three

Another section almost out of the way, and not a bad little one either. Not too long, and loads of blood and gore to keep your head off the desk. Some of it could even be useful some day — when someone's unconscious, you'll be glad you worked your way through it... So what are you waiting for... As always, keep going through them till you can answer every question without cheating.

1) Give three reasons why a warm-up is an important part of an exercise session, and two reasons why you should always do a cool-down.

2) Name four principles of training, and explain briefly what each one means.

3) Name four stages that a year's training can be broken into.
   What are the important features of each stage?

4) Name the four 'FITT' factors that must be considered when designing a training programme.

5) Name the three kinds of strength and two kinds of weight training. Describe the differences between the types of weight training, and their advantages and disadvantages.

6) Describe what is meant by: a) pressure training, b) circuit training, c) continuous training, d) fartlek training, e) interval training. Give two advantages and two disadvantages of each of these methods.

7) Give three reasons why it's good to have a high level of aerobic fitness. Describe the three main tests for aerobic fitness. How can you measure your heart rate?

8) Describe how you can test: a) endurance, b) strength, c) balance, d) agility, e) speed.

9) Describe these flexibility tests: a) the Shoulder Lift Test, b) the Sit and Reach Test.

10) What do you call an injury caused by: a) a sudden stress, b) a stress over a long period of time?

11) List some precautions you could take before an activity to help avoid injury. What precautions could you take during and after an activity?

12) Define soft-tissue injuries and hard-tissue injuries.

13) Injuries are divided into two types depending on whether you see blood.
    What are the two types called?

14) Explain exactly what these are: a) bruises, b) strains, c) sprains, and d) dislocations.

15) Why is the area around a fracture usually bruised?

16) What is a stress fracture? What causes it?

17) What's the RICE method? What injuries can you treat with it?
    What injuries shouldn't you treat with it?

18) What are the symptoms of hypothermia and hyperthermia? How should you treat them?

19) What causes cramp, winding and stitches? How should you treat them?

20) How should you treat concussion?

21) What is shock, and how should you treat it?

22) If you find someone unconscious, what are the first five things you should check?

23) How should you treat an unconscious casualty if they:
    a) are breathing, b) have a pulse but aren't breathing, c) don't have a pulse?

24) Describe how to give mouth-to-mouth ventilation and cardiac massage.

25) What position should you leave an unconscious casualty in while you go for help?
    (Give its name and describe it.) What are the benefits of this position?

26) Define a 'skill'. What's the difference between a basic skill and a complex one?

27) What is an open skill? And a closed one?

28) Describe a model of how your brain processes information. Draw a quick sketch to illustrate it. What are the main stages in the model?

29) What is selective attention, and what are its advantages?

30) What's the difference between intrinsic and extrinsic motivation? Give examples of each.

31) Describe the Inverted U Theory of arousal.

32) Name seven principles of goal setting.

Leisure and Recreation

You get to do what you <u>want</u> in leisure time, instead of doing your chores and stuff — it's great. And people now have <u>more leisure time</u> than they did a while back — so it's even more important.

Leisure Time and Recreation

Most of our time is taken up by things that <u>need</u> to be done:

1 SOCIAL DUTIES — going to school or work, and doing chores and things.

2 BODILY NEEDS — mainly eating and sleeping.

In the time that's left, we can <u>choose</u> what we want to do. This is our leisure time.

> **LEISURE** IS FREE TIME, WHEN YOU'RE NOT MEETING BODILY OR SOCIAL NEEDS.

Loads of people spend their leisure time doing some kind of <u>recreation</u>...

> **RECREATION** IS SOMETHING YOU DO IN YOUR LEISURE TIME BECAUSE YOU WANT TO.

DIFFERENCES BETWEEN SPORT AND PHYSICAL RECREATION

SPORTS are more <u>competitive</u> — they have <u>rules</u>, and the aim is always to <u>win</u>. Sports have <u>organised</u> events and competitions.

PHYSICAL RECREATION <u>isn't</u> as competitive — you're not competing against anyone but <u>yourself</u>, so you can set your own rules.

People Have More and More Leisure Time

LEISURE TIME IS INCREASING — people have <u>loads more leisure time</u> than they did fifty years ago due to:

1 <u>Less time working</u> — the working week is much shorter, and holidays are longer.

2 <u>Retiring earlier</u> — more people are taking early retirement.

3 More <u>unemployment</u> — largely due to jobs being taken over by machines.

4 <u>Machines</u> helping with <u>household chores</u> — e.g. washing machines, vacuum cleaners, dishwashers. They've gradually become <u>better</u>, <u>cheaper</u> and more widely <u>available</u>.

As people's leisure time increases, so does the <u>demand for facilities</u> and services to help fill that time. There's been huge <u>growth</u> in the '<u>leisure industry</u>' in recent years — and it's likely to continue.

More free time? — Not until you've finished revising...

Imagine you had no leisure time — you'd be at school all day. And after that, you'd have chores to do until it was time for bed. Things used to be like that (kind of), but now everyone has more leisure time. So you can use it all learning this page. Hooray for recreation...

Participation in Sport

The decision about <u>what sports to play</u> is affected by many things, including the people around you.

People are **Influenced** by the **Attitudes** of Others

Your <u>family and friends</u> can have a big influence on <u>whether</u> you do sport, and <u>which</u> sports you choose.

SUPPORT FROM FAMILY

1) <u>Parents</u> can <u>encourage</u> their children to take up sports.

2) Some sports need special <u>clothing</u> or <u>equipment</u>. It's usually parents who fork out the <u>cash</u>.

3) Many children <u>can't</u> easily get to and from sporting activities. They often <u>rely</u> on their parents to <u>get them there</u>.

4) Parents can also provide <u>coaching</u>.

PEER PRESSURE

1) Most people have a group of <u>friends</u> they spend much of their leisure time with. This group of friends is their <u>peer group</u>.

2) "The <u>individual's</u> behaviour and attitude can be <u>affected</u> by the <u>group's</u> behaviour and attitude." To say that in a less fancy way — "If <u>all your mates</u> play and like football, you'll <u>probably</u> play and like football."

3) "If a group's attitude towards sport is <u>negative</u>, then it's <u>harder</u> for <u>individuals</u> within the group to find opportunities to play sports." In a less fancy way — "If all your mates say that sport is <u>rubbish</u> and don't play it, <u>you'll do less sport</u>."

Schools have a Big Role in **Encouraging Sport**

Your <u>school</u> can be just as important as your family and friends when it comes to sport:

1) Schools have a very big role to play in <u>generating interest</u> in sport — and if you enjoy sports at <u>school</u> you're <u>more likely</u> to take them up when you <u>leave</u>.

2) <u>PE teachers</u> can affect your attitude towards sport and PE. A good teacher can build up your <u>confidence</u>, identify your <u>strengths</u> and <u>potential</u>, make the activity <u>enjoyable</u> and provide <u>coaching</u>.

3) Schools introduce you to a <u>wide range</u> of different activities, teaching the <u>basic skills</u> which you can build on later. The <u>National Curriculum</u> sets out the <u>minimum amount</u> that all schools have to teach, but many schools will also offer examination courses, extra-curricular activities, proficiency testing and various other awards. Some PE might be taught as part of <u>other subjects</u> too — e.g. health awareness.

4) As well as actually taking part, there are numerous <u>other sporting roles</u> you might have the chance to adopt. These include <u>official</u>, <u>observer</u>, <u>coach</u>, <u>captain</u>, <u>leader</u>, <u>organiser</u> and <u>choreographer</u>.

5) A school might give you access to <u>sports facilities</u> you won't find elsewhere, as well as <u>ICT equipment</u>. They might also have sporting <u>clubs and societies</u>, and <u>links</u> with local sports clubs.

I never knew that PE teachers were so important...

Just think — if it wasn't for schools, you wouldn't have to learn all about how schools encourage sport. Learning about the role of PE as part of your PE GCSE — the circularity is making me dizzy. Anyway, this is all important stuff, so cover the page and see how many of the points you can scribble down...

Participation in Sport

This page has the best mnemonic ever. Wait for it... ...SPAMFACET!

SPAMFACET — Other things affecting the Sports We Choose

S **SEX** — It's hard for <u>women</u> to get involved in a lot of sports which people still consider '<u>male sports</u>' — e.g. football, rugby, cricket.

P **POLITICS** — Politics has a big effect on the availability of <u>large-scale sporting</u> and <u>training facilities</u>, and also on what sports are taught or played in <u>schools</u>. It can also make sports illegal.

The government has recently banned hunting with dogs.

A **AGE** — Some sports are more popular with certain <u>age groups</u>. Most people aged <u>16-30</u> have <u>loads of choice</u> for sport, but more will choose to play <u>tennis</u>, say, rather than something like <u>bowls</u>. People <u>over 50</u> are more <u>limited</u> physically in the sports they can choose — so they tend to do <u>less strenuous</u> activities like walking or swimming.

M **MONEY** — Learning an activity like <u>skiing</u> isn't easy for most people in this country. Sports like this are more popular with <u>wealthy people</u> who can <u>afford</u> to go abroad to ski. Similarly many sports require <u>expensive equipment</u> which a lot of people couldn't afford.

F **FASHION** — Sports or leisure activities can go <u>in</u> or <u>out of fashion</u>. In the 1980s, <u>snooker</u> and <u>squash</u> became very popular. In the 90s, <u>aerobics</u> became very fashionable with endless tedious celebrity fitness videos being released. <u>Media coverage</u> of sports can have a big effect on sporting fashions.

A **ACCEPTABILITY** — Some sports are considered <u>socially unacceptable</u> by some people — e.g. they might object to off-road driving because of <u>environmental concerns</u>, or horse racing because of <u>cruelty to animals</u>.

C **CHALLENGE/DANGER** — Many people are attracted to sports with an element of <u>risk</u>, like climbing or motor racing. They wouldn't get the same <u>stimulation</u> and <u>enjoyment</u> from something like bowls.

E **ENVIRONMENT/CLIMATE/ACCESS** — The <u>area you live in</u> affects the sports you choose — there's more <u>opportunity</u> for outdoor activities like hillwalking, rock-climbing or windsurfing in the Lake District than in the sprawling metropolis of Manchester.

T **TECHNOLOGY** — Technology affects the <u>availability</u>, <u>cost</u> and <u>safety</u> of equipment, materials and facilities. It can also lead to improved <u>teaching</u> and <u>training aids</u>, which might encourage more participation.

If everyone takes part, there won't be any left...

This little lot shouldn't be too hard to learn — just so long as you can recall those key words. But do test yourself to make sure you really do know it. And you know what that means — cover the page and scribble everything down. SPAMFACET should give you your headings...

Women in Sport

There used to be a lot of stupid and <u>bigoted</u> views that stopped female participation in sport — held by <u>both</u> men and women. We've come on a <u>long way</u>, but things still <u>aren't equal</u>.

Women used to be Discouraged from doing Sport

Compared to nowadays, people used to think very <u>differently</u> about women in sport — they thought that:

1. <u>Physical activity</u> was something to be done by <u>men only</u> and that it made women look very <u>unattractive</u>.

2. Women could <u>harm themselves</u> by doing too much physical activity.

3. Women should wear '<u>respectable</u>' clothing that <u>covered their bodies up</u> (e.g. long dresses). This meant that playing sport was very <u>uncomfortable</u>.

4. Women should look after the <u>home</u> and the <u>children</u> — this meant they didn't have the <u>time</u> or energy to play sport.

<u>Attitudes</u> to women in sport are much <u>better</u> today. <u>More</u> and <u>more</u> women are playing sport because they <u>aren't</u> being <u>held back</u>. <u>Local authorities</u> often have <u>women-only</u> evenings at gyms and swimming pools as an incentive for women to join in. They provide a <u>relaxing</u> environment for women to <u>meet people</u> with similar interests, while they get plenty of <u>exercise</u> at the same time.

Women's Sport tends to have a Lower Profile

Despite all this progress, women's sport still faces problems.

PROBLEMS FACING WOMEN'S SPORT

1) Too many sports are still considered '<u>male only</u>'.

2) Women are often <u>not allowed</u> to compete <u>with men</u>. This is even true in sports like snooker where factors like physical strength have <u>no relevance</u>. <u>Showjumping</u> is one of the few events where women can compete against men.

3) <u>Poor media coverage</u> — women's events usually have a <u>lower profile</u> than men's events.

4) <u>Less sponsorship</u> — companies want to sponsor the events with the <u>most media attention</u> — generally the <u>men's events</u>.

5) <u>Less prize money</u> — women's events usually have less prize money than men's events — <u>even</u> in sports where the women do get <u>good media coverage</u> (e.g. tennis).

6) <u>Few role models</u> for women — again, lack of <u>media</u> support is the main problem.

Women's Sport is now Promoted

WOMEN'S SPORTS FOUNDATION — set up in 1984 in the UK. It aims to:

1) Increase <u>awareness</u> of the <u>issues</u> surrounding women in sport.

2) Help girls and women to get involved in sport at <u>all levels</u>.

3) Encourage <u>organisations</u> to improve sporting opportunities for women.

4) <u>Challenge inequality</u> in sport and seek to bring about <u>change</u>.

5) Raise the <u>profile</u> of British sportswomen.

It's hard to play football in a big dress...

So as you can see, women really do get a rotten deal when it comes to sport. Remember — the stuff at the top of the page about attitudes towards women is what many people used to think, it's hopefully not how many people think today. There are lots of juicy points here — learn 'em.

Sporting Behaviour

The behaviour of both players and spectators has a big effect on any competition. You need to know about this behaviour, and how hooliganism can cause problems for sport.

Etiquette — *The **Unwritten** Rules*

The rules of any sport are written down — but etiquette is like an unwritten code of behaviour.

ETIQUETTE IN SPORTS

Etiquette in sport means fair play and good manners. It makes life better for everybody. For example:

1) Football players often kick the ball out of play if an opponent is injured — so they can be treated. At the throw-in, the team that kicked the ball out should be given the ball back.

2) At the end of a tennis match, players should shake their opponent's and the umpire's hand.

At the other end of the scale, gamesmanship (or 'psyching out' your opponent) is behaviour that's very close to cheating.

VIOLENCE BETWEEN PLAYERS

1) Violence between competitors is rare in non-contact sports like athletics (where there's no direct aggression).

2) Fights do break out in aggressive team sports like rugby and ice hockey.

3) Some people say that violence among players causes spectator violence — but no one has proved or disproved this.

4) If a player has behaved violently, they can be fined or suspended (not allowed to play for a certain time) by the governing body — and their club can be fined.

Spectators have their **Good** Points and **Bad** Points

Having lots of spectators is an advantage for any club — but there is a downside.

THE UPSIDE OF SPECTATORS

1) Crowds can influence a match — cheering on their team and putting off the opponents. This is one reason why playing at home is an advantage.

2) They buy tickets and other club merchandise (like shirts and scarves), which brings revenue (money) into a club.

THE DOWNSIDE OF SPECTATORS

1) Facilities are needed, and marshals have to be provided to supervise crowds.

2) The police may be needed to control large crowds — and clubs have to pay for this.

3) Hooliganism can be a problem.

Bad behaviour ruins sport — it's just not cricket...

Jolly good show, well done. Another page under your belt... ...or is it? Are you sure you know all about etiquette? Are you positive that you've got all the advantages and disadvantages of spectators properly lodged in your brain? Read it once more for luck...

Hooliganism

It seems not a season goes by when you don't hear something about badly behaved football fans causing trouble. Well, here's how <u>hooliganism</u> has shaped the way that people watch football today.

Football Disasters Led to the *Taylor Report*

There are a lot of <u>theories</u> about why hooliganism has become such a problem in football. Possible <u>causes</u> include changes in <u>society</u>, increasing <u>commercialism</u> within the game and the attitude and behaviour of the <u>players</u>. Many people link hooliganism to <u>alcohol</u>.

Hooliganism has contributed to several <u>disasters</u>, in which fans were killed. Action had to be taken to try to solve the problem.

THE HEYSEL DISASTER

At the European Cup Final in <u>1985</u>, 39 Juventus fans were <u>killed</u> when Liverpool supporters rushed towards them, making a <u>wall collapse</u>.

THE HILLSBOROUGH DISASTER

At the <u>1989</u> FA Cup semi-final, 96 fans were <u>crushed</u> to death against fences round the pitch, after <u>too many people</u> had been let in to the stadium.

After these two disasters, the <u>Taylor Report</u> suggested ways to make stadiums <u>safer</u>.

The *Taylor Report* Recommended Major Changes to Football

1) Stadiums had to have <u>fences</u> to separate opposing fans.

2) Stadiums in some divisions had to become '<u>all-seater</u>' — there could be no more terraces full of people standing.

3) Club <u>membership schemes</u> were introduced, so known troublemakers could be <u>barred</u> from entering grounds.

4) <u>Perimeter fences</u> between crowds and the pitch were <u>removed</u>.

5) <u>Closed circuit TV</u> (CCTV) around stadiums now monitors fans.

6) <u>Information</u> is now <u>shared</u> by police forces in different countries.

Tragic events led to safer football grounds...

The Heysel and Hillsborough disasters, and the Taylor Report that followed, were very important — so you should learn all about them. Make sure you learn ALL the recommendations of the Taylor Report. There's only six of them — it won't take you long...

Warm-Up and Worked Exam Questions

Warm-up Questions

1) What is leisure?
2) What is recreation?
3) What sets out the minimum amount of sporting activities that a school must teach?
4) Give two problems faced by women's sport.
5) "An unwritten code of behaviour in sport." What is this describing?
6) In which year did the Heysel Disaster take place?

Worked Exam Questions

You know the drill — have a careful look through the worked examples, then have a go at some questions yourself on the next page. Check you got them right before you move on.

1   Polly enjoys sport and is keen to compete in as many different activities as possible.

a)   Name one activity where she can compete against men.

Showjumping

(1 mark)

b)   Give two problems facing women's sport and two ways in which the Women's Sports Foundation is helping.

Problems — few role models, lack of sponsorship/prize money

Help — Women's Sports Foundation is working to increase

awareness of the issues surrounding women in sport and raise

the profile of British sportswomen.

4 marks available — so that's 2 marks for the problems   *(4 marks)*
and 2 marks for the ways the WSF is helping.

2   Schools play a big role in sport.

a)   Name two sporting roles (besides playing) you may be able to adopt at school.

Official   *There are loads of possible answers —*
                    choreographer, linesman, captain, etc...
Coach

(2 marks)

b)   List two factors that may affect the sports you choose.

The amount of money you have.

Politics — e.g. what sports the government encourages in schools.

Remember SPAMFACET!   *(2 marks)*

Exam Questions

1   Jack and his friends regularly support their local football team.

    a)   Explain how sports clubs can benefit from having spectators, and give two
        problems that spectators can cause.

        ....

        ....

        ....

        ....

(4 marks)

    b)   What measures did the Taylor Report recommend?

        ....

        ....

        ....

(3 marks)

2   Explain the difference between sport and physical recreation.

    ....

    ....

(2 marks)

3   John is 60 and plays badminton regularly.

    a)   Why might he have a lot of leisure time?

        ....

(1 mark)

    b)   How might his age affect the sport he plays?

        ....

(1 mark)

    c)   Discuss two other factors that might have affected John's choice of sport.

        ....

        ....

        ....

        ....

(4 marks)

Local Sports Clubs

There are loads of <u>rules</u> to be followed and <u>organising</u> to be done if you want to play sport.
Local <u>sports clubs</u> help their members with the <u>boring stuff</u>, so people can get on with playing.

Most Local Sports Clubs have a similar **Structure**

Local sports clubs often have a <u>structure</u> like the one below.

THE MEMBERS — usually <u>pay</u> to join the club. They <u>elect</u> the committee.

COMMITTEE — elected by the members to <u>run the club</u>.

CHAIRPERSON — the <u>top official</u> who represents the club and chairs the meetings.

VICE-CHAIRPERSON — takes over if the chairperson is away.

TREASURER — manages the club's <u>finances</u>.

SECRETARY — does all the <u>boring jobs</u>, like taking notes at meetings, and letting all the members know what's going on.

MEMBERSHIP SECRETARY — tries to <u>enrol new members</u> so the club can keep going.

FIXTURES SECRETARY — <u>organises club events</u>, both competitive (e.g. matches) and non-competitive (e.g. dinners).

COACH — helps all club members to train, and coaches the club team.

Local Sports Clubs are for the **Members**

LOCAL SPORTS CLUBS — deal with:

1) <u>Administration</u> — the paperwork and organisation needed to run the club.
2) <u>Facilities</u> — maintaining the playing, changing and social areas and equipment.
3) <u>Competition</u> — running competitions within the club, or against other clubs.
4) <u>Coaching</u> — helping its members improve their skills, and encouraging juniors to play.

There are three main types of **Competition**

A lot of sport's about competition, let's face it. These are the main ways competitions are organised:

1) **LEAGUE** — Each team or player plays against <u>all the others</u> at least once (often twice — home and away). They get <u>points</u> for winning or drawing a game. The winner is the player or team with the most points at the end of the season. Leagues are a <u>very fair</u> way to run a competition, because they reward <u>consistency</u> over a long time. The trouble is they <u>may take too long</u>, and if there are too many people or teams they may have to be divided up into smaller leagues.

2) **KNOCK-OUT** — It's played in <u>rounds</u>, with each player or team playing one game per round. They <u>go through</u> to the next round if they <u>win</u>, otherwise they're out of the competition. Knock-outs are <u>easy to organise</u> and <u>quick to run</u>, but they're <u>not as fair</u>, as you only get one chance. On the other hand, they're <u>more exciting</u> to watch and take part in.

3) **LADDER** — The players are listed on a ladder. Each can <u>challenge</u> a player higher on the ladder, but only up to a certain number of rungs higher. If they <u>beat</u> them, they <u>take their place</u> on the ladder. This is no good for <u>team sports</u> and can be <u>demoralising</u> for new players who must start at the bottom.

Even sport has paperwork — in your case, exam papers...

Phew! There's some stuff on this page alright. That sports club structure is a toughy. The easiest way to get it stuck in your head is to fill in all the positions with real people from a real club...

Sporting Facilities

You might not need good <u>facilities</u> for most sports — but it definitely makes playing them <u>easier</u>. You've got to know about the <u>differences</u> between facilities, and the <u>problems</u> of planning them.

There are *Indoor* and *Outdoor* Sports Facilities

OUTDOOR FACILITIES — including <u>pitches</u> (e.g. for football, rugby, cricket), <u>tracks</u> (e.g. for athletics, motor racing, horse racing), facilities for <u>water sports</u> (e.g. outdoor swimming pool), and <u>natural features</u> (e.g. for cross-country running, canoeing).

INDOOR FACILITIES — usually <u>purpose-built</u> buildings such as swimming pools and sports halls (used for loads of sports, like tennis, basketball, badminton and football).

To Build Indoor Facilities You need to *Plan Ahead*

These are some examples of <u>questions</u> that should be asked when planning an indoor facility.

1. Are people going to <u>use</u> it?
2. Can people <u>park</u> there?
3. Can it be used for <u>other things</u>?
4. Can people <u>get to it</u>?
5. What impact will it have on the <u>environment</u>?
6. What will it <u>cost</u>?
7. Is there any <u>competition</u>? (from similar facilities nearby)

Both the *Public* and *Private* Sectors Provide Facilities

PUBLIC SECTOR FACILITIES

1) Owned by <u>local authorities</u> and <u>councils</u>.
2) Usually run at a <u>loss</u> (subsidised by taxes).
3) Examples include: sports pitches, leisure centres, swimming pools and sports halls.

PRIVATE SECTOR FACILITIES

1) Owned by <u>companies</u> or <u>individuals</u>.
2) Run to <u>make money</u> or break even.
3) Examples include: sports stadiums (e.g. Wembley), tennis clubs, golf clubs, football stadiums and health clubs.
4) Include <u>voluntarily</u> run facilities, e.g. football, rugby and golf clubs, and things like church halls.

CENTRES OF EXCELLENCE

Offer really <u>good</u> facilities for the <u>best athletes</u>:

1) <u>Crystal Palace</u> (athletics, swimming, and martial arts),
2) <u>Bisham Abbey</u> (tennis),
3) <u>Lilleshall</u> (football),
4) <u>Holme Pierrepoint</u> (water sports),
5) <u>Plas-y-Brenin</u> (outdoor activities),
6) <u>National Cycling Centre</u>.

Map Showing the Centres of Excellence

Facilities, what can you say — er... really important...
Most of this stuff is common sense and general knowledge. Learn the three main headings first of all.

Sporting Bodies and Organisations

Sporting bodies <u>encourage</u> and <u>help</u> people to play sport. There are <u>loads</u> and loads of them, all across the world. But don't worry — you only need to know about the ones on these two pages.

National Governing Bodies of Sport have **Four Main Roles**

GOVERNING BODIES — their <u>four</u> main roles are:

1) To maintain the <u>rules</u> of the sport and keep <u>discipline</u> (e.g. by fining or banning competitors).

2) To <u>promote</u> the sport.

3) To organise <u>international</u> competitive events, and run the <u>national team</u>.

4) To organise <u>national</u> competitions.

Examples of the UK's sporting governing bodies are the <u>FA</u> (Football Association) and <u>UKA</u> (UK Athletics).

UK Sport — Used to be the Sports Council

In 1997 '<u>UK Sport</u>' was made from the old 'Sports Council'.
It was set up to produce <u>top sporting performers</u> in the UK.

UK SPORT — aims to:

1) Give the UK's world-class performers <u>excellent support</u>.

2) Improve the UK's <u>profile</u> and <u>influence</u> on the international sporting stage.

3) Promote <u>ethical</u> behaviour and provide an <u>anti-doping</u> programme.

4) Persuade governing bodies that the UK is the best place to hold <u>major sporting events</u> and that UK Sport can run them.

Each <u>Home Country</u> has its own sports council too: Sports Council for Wales; Sports Council for Northern Ireland; Sport Scotland; Sport England.

HOME COUNTRY COUNCILS — aim to:

1) Increase <u>participation</u> in sports.

2) Improve the number and quality of <u>facilities</u>.

3) Improve sporting <u>standards</u>.

4) Allocate <u>lottery funding</u>.

Central Council for Physical Recreation — CCPR

The CCPR is a <u>voluntary umbrella organisation</u> for the <u>governing bodies</u> of all the different sports in Britain. It tries to:

1) <u>Encourage</u> sport and physical recreation.

2) Advise its members on <u>legal</u> and <u>financial</u> issues.

3) Give <u>advice</u> about British sport to other bodies and authorities.

4) Develop <u>award schemes</u> (e.g. the Sports Leader Awards, which is run by their charitable arm, the British Sports Trust).

CCPR — is funded by:

1 <u>Donations</u> from its members.

2 <u>Sponsorship</u>.

3 A <u>grant</u> from the <u>UK Sports Council</u>.

4 <u>Sales</u> of books, magazines and other things.

So many bodies — and that's only the half of it... *(there's more on the next page)*

There are three types of council to get to grips with — UK Sport, Home Country councils and the CCPR. Learn what they do and how they're different. It's not exciting, but it is important.

Sporting Bodies and Organisations

You've got to know about <u>all</u> these organisations, and what they <u>do</u>. It won't be as exciting as downhill skiing, but it beats the hell out of maths (allegedly). Get it <u>learnt</u> or chuck away marks.

International Olympic Committee — IOC

INTERNATIONAL OLYMPIC COMMITTEE (IOC)

1) <u>Runs</u> the Olympics.
2) Selects <u>where</u> the games are held.
3) Decides <u>which sports</u> are included.
4) Helps to <u>plan</u> the games.
5) Fights against <u>doping</u> and <u>corruption</u> in sport.

British Olympic Association — BOA

BRITISH OLYMPIC ASSOCIATION (BOA)

1) Organises the <u>British Olympic Team</u>.
2) <u>Raises money</u> so the team can compete at the Olympics.
3) Works with governing bodies of sport to help the athletes <u>prepare</u> for the Olympics.
4) Coordinates <u>British bids</u> to host the Games.

Sports Coach UK (used to be the National Coaching Foundation)

SPORTS COACH UK

1) Works to improve the <u>quality of coaching</u> in the UK.
2) Helps the education and development of <u>coaches</u>.
3) Is concerned with <u>all levels</u> of coaching at all ages.

Sports Aid Foundation — SAF

SPORTS AID FOUNDATION (SAF)

1) <u>Raises money</u> to help athletes who can't <u>afford</u> to train or compete.
2) Gets money from <u>National Lottery</u> donations, <u>sponsorship</u> and <u>grants</u>.

Countryside Commission — CC

COUNTRYSIDE COMMISSION (CC)

1) Looks after the <u>countryside</u>.
2) <u>Advises</u> authorities like the government on countryside issues.
3) Ensures the countryside is used for <u>physical recreation</u>.
4) Ensures the countryside is <u>protected</u>.
5) Set up the <u>Country Code</u>.

So many acronyms — make sure you know what they stand for...

How can we possibly need so many organisations? Learn exactly what each one does, then you'll know.

Warm-Up and Worked Exam Questions

Warm-up Questions

1) What is the role of the treasurer of a club?
2) In what type of competition does each team play all the others — ladder, league or knock-out?
3) Is Holme Pierrepoint an indoor or an outdoor facility?
4) Who owns a public sector facility — a company, council, local authority or an individual?
5) What do the initials IOC stand for?
6) Who supports the UK's world-class performers?

Worked Exam Questions

Take a look over these examples, then try some exam-style questions yourself.

1 Billy is a member of the EBBA (English Basketball Association).

a) The EBBA is an example of what type of organisation?

It's one of the UK's national governing bodies.

The organisation has 'English' and a sport in its name,
so it's likely to be a national governing body.   *(1 mark)*

b) Identify three of the main roles of the EBBA.

Maintain the rules and discipline of the sport.

Promote the sport.

Organise national competitions and run the national team.

You don't need to know anything about the EBBA to answer this   *(3 marks)*
question — all national governing bodies perform these functions.

2 Jessica wants to join her local badminton club.

a) Which committee member should she speak to?

The membership secretary

   (1 mark)

b) Jessica joined the club and was invited to play in their ladder competition.
Explain how this type of competition works.

Players are listed on a "ladder". You can challenge any player

who occupies a position up to a specific number of rungs above

you. If you beat them, you take their place on the ladder.

   (3 marks)

Exam Questions

1   The local council wants to build a new leisure centre on the outskirts of town.

a)   Identify four things they will need to consider during the planning stage.

....

....

....

(4 marks)

b)   The new centre is a public sector facility. What is the difference between a public sector and private sector facility? Give an example of each.

....

....

....

....

(4 marks)

2   Many cities submitted bids to host the 2012 Olympics, including London.

a)   Which organisation is responsible for UK bids?

....

(1 mark)

b)   Describe the main roles of the IOC (International Olympic Committee).

....

....

....

....

(4 marks)

3   Rosie has been asked to attend the European Student Archery Championships in Rome. She will need to pay for her travel.

a)   Where can she go for help with funding her trip?

....

(1 mark)

b)   What other organisation could help Rosie if she wanted to become a world-class competitor?

....

(1 mark)

Finance of Sport

You only have to look at what <u>Manchester United's</u> top player gets a week to see
that there's a <u>shed-load</u> of money at the top end of sport.
At the other end of the scale, the amateur players in "Jingleberry United" have to
pay a <u>club fee</u> and <u>match fee</u> before they can play in the glorious Sunday League.

Amateur Sport is Run on Very Little Money

See also p103.

<u>Amateurs</u> take part in sports for <u>fun</u> — not as a <u>profession</u>.

PUBLIC FACILITIES

Public sports facilities (e.g.
public swimming pools) are
subsidised by the <u>local council</u>
to keep prices for the public
<u>low</u>. Local councils get money
for this from <u>local taxes</u>.

PRIVATE FACILITIES

Private facilities
often <u>charge</u> a lot
to cover their cost
and make a <u>profit</u>.

SPONSORSHIP

At the local level <u>small
businesses</u> sponsor local
teams. This generally
involves <u>buying</u> the
shirts and sticking their
<u>name</u> on them.

Small Amateur Clubs

& Recreational Sport

SMALL SPORTS CLUBS

Small sports clubs cover the costs of
things like court hire and equipment with
<u>membership fees</u>. Teams from these clubs
pay <u>match fees</u> to cover the cost of
entering the league. <u>Gambling levies</u> can
also be a big source of income for
voluntary clubs — e.g. from <u>raffles</u>.

NATIONAL LOTTERY FUNDING

Groups can <u>apply</u> for lottery funding
to build or improve sports facilities
in an area. The <u>competition</u> for
National Lottery funding is <u>fierce</u>
and the applicants must have raised
at least <u>half</u> the money themselves.

Amateur clubs have it tough...

Here you go — a nice easy page to learn. Only a swift five points to cram into your cranium. Go on,
you can squeeze them in. It's important that you're able to explain where amateur sport gets its funding
from — it's just the kind of thing they might ask in the exam...

Finance of Sport

Professional sportsmen and sportswomen get paid for taking part. As I'm sure you all know, professional sport is where the big money is. If you fancy making your fortune as a sports star, the most lucrative sports to try are football, golf or tennis. Or Formula 1 (though I found the equipment a bit pricey)...

Professional Sport needs a Lot of Money

See also p103.

Popular sports and the people who play them at the top level can expect a load of money. But it ain't all big bucks and fast cars — less popular sports and their players must work hard to get the money they need.

TV and Radio

TV companies pay whopping amounts for the rights to show the biggest sporting events. The governing body of the sport involved gets that dosh. They use it to promote and develop their sport. Large companies get very excited and throw loads of sponsorship money at people and teams that get on the telly.

Sponsorship and Merchandising

For big clubs and teams sponsorship means a heck of a lot more than a couple of shirts and a round of sandwiches. They can also rake in the money through sales of replica shirts and other such merchandise. It ain't as easy for people in lesser known sports like gymnastics where people have to pay their own way a lot of the time.

Grants

Up-and-coming sports stars can apply for funding from the Sports Aid Foundation (SAF) to cover the cost of their transport, training etc. The SAF gets money from donations and fund-raising. The British Olympic Association (BOA) covers the cost for the British Olympic team with money from fund-raising and commercial sponsorship. See page 96 for more on the SAF and BOA.

Competitions

Small scale competitions that don't command media attention have to rely on entrance fees to cover their costs. Larger events can cover costs through sponsorship — and an event like the Olympics can make a boat-full of money.

Four ways to make big money — and get big marks...

Another easy page. Don't get all cocky and just skim through it though — these points are vital to understanding how sport is funded. When you get to my age, you begin to realise just how important money is. What would have happened if Kelly Holmes hadn't had £50 for a new pair of trainers?

Sponsorship

Sponsorship exists to give good <u>publicity</u> to the sponsors. Sponsorship funds sports, teams or individuals in part or in full. The <u>more famous</u> the sport, team or individual, the <u>higher</u> the payout.

Everything is Sponsored *from the Team to the Ball*

If people are going to <u>see it</u>, companies will slap their <u>name</u> on it, whether it's a person, team, league, stand, trophy, mascot, badge, or ball. This means big bucks for the <u>famous few</u>.

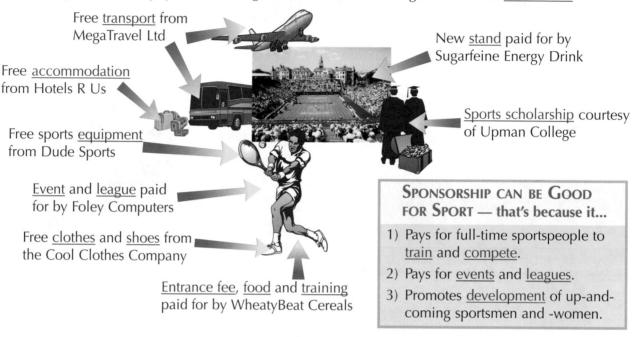

Free <u>transport</u> from MegaTravel Ltd

Free <u>accommodation</u> from Hotels R Us

Free sports <u>equipment</u> from Dude Sports

<u>Event</u> and <u>league</u> paid for by Foley Computers

Free <u>clothes</u> and <u>shoes</u> from the Cool Clothes Company

<u>Entrance fee</u>, <u>food</u> and <u>training</u> paid for by WheatyBeat Cereals

New <u>stand</u> paid for by Sugarfeine Energy Drink

<u>Sports scholarship</u> courtesy of Upman College

SPONSORSHIP CAN BE GOOD FOR SPORT — that's because it...

1) Pays for full-time sportspeople to <u>train</u> and <u>compete</u>.
2) Pays for <u>events</u> and <u>leagues</u>.
3) Promotes <u>development</u> of up-and-coming sportsmen and -women.

Sponsors *get a lot out of Sponsorship Too*

<u>Why</u> do sponsors give away all that dosh? Read on and learn their devious ways...

1) **FREE ADVERTISING** — See a good player using it and you'll want to use it.
2) **IMAGE** — The company becomes associated with winners.
3) **SCHOLARSHIPS** — Some universities and colleges offer places (at discounted grades) to students who excel at particular sports. In return universities gain prestige for sporting excellence.
4) **TAX AND HOSPITALITY** — Sponsors don't usually have to pay tax on the money they spend on sponsorship. They also get free tickets to the events they sponsor, which they can use to impress clients and employees.
5) **AREN'T THEY NICE** — Companies often sponsor charity and local events. Whether this is out of the kindness of their hearts or to improve their corporate image is by the by.

There is a **Negative** *side to Sponsorship*

It's not all 'fun in the sun' when it comes to sponsorship — this lot covers the bad bits.

1) <u>Not everyone</u> can get sponsorship — companies <u>aren't interested</u> in sponsoring people from sports which <u>aren't popular</u>.
2) It could all <u>turn nasty</u> — get <u>injured</u>, lose your <u>form</u> or get a bad <u>reputation</u> and it's bye–bye sponsorship deal.
3) <u>Abuse of power</u> — associating cigarettes and alcohol with sport gives a <u>false</u> image of health.

CGP CGP CGP CGP *(CGP — Official Sponsors of page 101)...*
Sponsorship's a good way of getting money into sport. It might look like a win-win situation for everyone, but it does have downsides. Make sure you know who gets what out of it, and who gets nowt.

Sport and the Media

You <u>can't avoid sport</u> — it's there in the daily papers, on the radio, in books, in films, on the Internet. Choose any type of media and there it is. Which is great for me 'cos I <u>love it</u>.

Sport turns up Everywhere from **Papers** to the **Internet**

1) **TV** and **Radio**
2) **Cable** and **Satellite** — pay-per-view events
3) **Ceefax** and **Teletext**
4) **Internet**
5) **Newspapers** and **Magazines**
6) **Books** and **Films**

SPORTS PROGRAMMES:
Live sport, highlights, quiz shows, documentaries, news.

SPORTS ARTICLES:
Sports results/predictions, behind the scenes, players' private lives, biographies.

The media coverage of sport relies heavily on <u>technology</u>. Apart from making all these forms of coverage possible, it also improves them with things like <u>instant replays</u>, <u>photo finishes</u>, <u>underwater cameras</u>, <u>split times</u>, and timing to hundredths or <u>thousandths of seconds</u>.

The **Media** has a **Good Effect** on Sport...

The coverage of sport in the media does good stuff for sport.

MONEY — Media companies <u>pay</u> for the rights to show a sport — <u>sponsorship</u> for a sport will also <u>increase dramatically</u> if it's popularised by the media.

EDUCATION — People learn about the <u>rules and tactics</u> of sports.

DAVID BECKHAM — (OK I couldn't think of a good 'D'.) Produces <u>role models</u> for people to aspire to. If the role models stay good, everything's fine and dandy.

INSPIRATION — Brings sport to people who may not experience it otherwise. This can <u>encourage participation</u>.

AID TO COACHING — Sport on TV and video lets you <u>study the performance</u> of others.

...and a **Bad Effect** on Sport

The media does lots of <u>good</u> for sport...
...but it has a <u>dark side</u> to it tooooooo....(that was supposed to sound eerie).

BIAS — Only the really popular spectator sports get plenty of coverage. Very <u>little coverage</u> is given to <u>less popular</u> sports, starving them of all the benefits shown above.

Replays have helped prosecute rugby players for stamping and other infringements.

LACK OF ATTENDANCE — Watching it live on telly means you're not at the game — <u>reducing ticket sales</u>, then the media 'steals' more of this money with 'pay-per-view' or channel subscription fees.

OVERLOAD — "SPORT, SPORT, SPORT! It's all that's on" — <u>too much sport</u>. (According to mum.)

OPEN SEASON — Sports stars are <u>hounded</u> by the media, who are quick to pounce if a sports superstar's halo slips.

DEMANDS TO COMPLY — The media actually <u>imposes rules</u> on sports to make them more <u>exciting</u>, e.g. <u>tie breaks</u> were introduced into tennis as a result of media pressure. The media can also dictate the <u>date and time</u> that a sporting event is held, in order to get the <u>maximum viewers</u>.

Too much sport? Well, this is GCSE PE — what did you expect?

Like with sponsorship, the media's involvement in sport isn't just a bed of roses. Learn what things sport relies on the media for, but know how it suffers from media coverage as well.

Amateurs and Professionals

It's dead important to know the <u>difference</u> between an amateur and a professional. It's all about <u>money</u> — professionals get paid but amateurs don't. All the info you need to learn is here.

Pros do it for Money — Amateurs for Love

You've got to know what the difference between an amateur and a professional is. It's easy.

AMATEURS — <u>don't get paid</u> for playing sport — they do it as a <u>hobby</u> because they <u>like it</u>.

PROFESSIONALS — <u>get paid</u> for playing their sport — it's their <u>full-time job</u>.

1) Some sports are <u>totally amateur</u>, e.g. hockey.

2) Others have professionals and amateurs who compete <u>separately</u>, e.g. football.

3) Others are <u>open</u> — everyone competes against everyone else, e.g. tennis.

Pros and Ams — It was all a Matter of Class

The <u>class system</u> had a lot to do with how sport was divided into amateurs and professionals.

<u>Amateurs</u> were <u>gentlemen</u> — from the wealthy upper classes. They could afford to play just for fun.

<u>Professionals</u> were from a <u>lower class</u>. They competed for money, often just doing things for a bet.

Sport's attitude towards professionals has <u>changed</u> over the years.

1) The <u>Olympics</u> were only supposed to be for <u>amateurs</u> — that was the original rule.

2) But people started to <u>bend</u> the rules — they got paid, but competed as <u>amateurs</u> so they could take part in the Olympics.

3) It was becoming <u>impossible</u> to decide who was a true amateur, so the word 'amateur' was <u>dropped</u> from the Olympic rule book.

4) <u>Governing bodies</u> and the <u>IOC</u> (International Olympic Committee) now <u>decide</u> who can compete in the Olympics.

1) The <u>Amateur Athletic Association</u> started up in 1880. No professionals could join.

2) Professional <u>football</u> became legal in 1884.

3) Rugby split into <u>two codes</u> in 1895 — Rugby League players could be paid, but Rugby Union players couldn't.

4) Money from <u>TV</u> companies and <u>sponsorship</u> means that professional athletes can now earn <u>£millions a year</u>.

People thought sport and money <u>didn't mix</u> — <u>gambling</u> on most sports was <u>banned</u> to discourage cheating.

Most sports didn't let amateurs and professionals compete together — but <u>cricket</u> did. <u>Amateurs</u> were 'gentlemen', and <u>professionals</u> 'players'. They usually played on the <u>same team</u> — but once a year they played against each other in the 'Gentlemen and Players' match.

Shamateurs — The Paid Amateurs

Amateur athletes wanted to find ways to <u>train full-time</u>, without being classed as professionals.

SCHOLARSHIPS — Colleges offer talented people the chance to <u>train full-time</u> for <u>free</u> — without doing much actual studying.

TRUST FUNDS — <u>Prize money</u> is paid into a trust fund. Athletes can take <u>living expenses</u> from the fund during their career — and get the rest when they <u>retire</u>.

SPONSORSHIP — e.g. athletes get paid for wearing a company's <u>logo</u> on their clothing.

'EXPENSES' PAYMENTS — These are often much <u>more</u> than what the athletes actually spend.

TOKEN 'JOBS' — Talented athletes can be given 'jobs' where they <u>don't have to do anything</u>, so they can train full-time.

GIFTS — Things like cars could be given as <u>presents</u>, and then <u>sold</u>.

ILLEGAL PAYMENTS — Nothing fancy here. Just take the cash and <u>keep quiet</u>.

I wish someone would give me a token job...   Make sure you know the stuff about the Olympics and cricket — it's dead important. The last section's also closely linked to the Olympics — and could easily be in an Olympic Games question in the exam.

International Sport

International competitions were first organised in the 19th century — and since then they've just got bigger and bigger. Learn about their pros and cons, and how attitudes towards them vary.

There are Loads of International Sporting Events

There are loads of international competitions. You should know a bit about some important ones...

THE OLYMPIC GAMES: Summer and winter competitions held every four years.

THE PAN-AMERICAN GAMES: Held every four years for countries in North, South or Central America.

THE COMMONWEALTH GAMES: Held every four years and open to countries in the Commonwealth (the group of countries that used to be in the British Empire).

WORLD CUPS: In cricket, rugby, football — all held every four years.

Nowadays, nearly every major sport has its own world championships.

Big International Competitions have Pros and Cons

These big tournaments all have their good points — but they can also cause problems.

ADVANTAGES

1) Players and supporters from different countries can meet, and experience different cultures and ways of life.

2) Competition between the best athletes in the world constantly pushes standards higher.

3) International events encourage people from all around the world to take part in sport.

DISADVANTAGES

1) Big tournaments are expensive to organise, so poor countries can't afford to stage them.

2) Not even rich countries are willing to host big competitions without help from big business — and this makes sport more commercialised.

3) Some countries want success at sport to 'prove' they are more successful than an enemy. The USA and USSR used to do this.

Different Countries have Different Attitudes to Sport

Every country wants success in sport — it gives status and pride, can bring a nation together and make people healthier. But different countries promote sport in different ways...

UNITED KINGDOM	USA	FORMER EASTERN BLOC	THIRD WORLD COUNTRIES
1) PE is compulsory in schools.	1) PE is compulsory in schools.	(The countries that were dominated by the USSR.)	1) Popular sport has to be cheap — football and athletics are booming.
2) Grants and sponsorship are available for promising talent.	2) School and college sport is high profile and attracts big sponsorship.	1) Sport was controlled by the state.	2) International success will earn money.
3) Some top competitors have trust funds.	3) Scholarship schemes help promising athletes.	2) Talented children were trained from a very young age — and then given token jobs in the army or industry.	3) Top athletes are often given token government jobs.
4) 'Sport for All' campaigns boost participation.	4) Top college athletes are drafted into professional leagues.	3) Sport has been more open since 1989.	

A London Olympics? Well, I'm not paying for it...

There's quite a lot here again. You won't really need to know much about individual competitions — just as long as you know they exist and can name a few of them. The most important bits are the pros and cons of hosting a major sporting event — so spend a bit more time on these.

The Olympic Games

The <u>Modern Olympic Games</u> have been around since 1896 — and they've <u>changed</u> quite a bit since then. You need to know a bit about the <u>history</u> of the games, and the <u>pros and cons</u> of playing <u>host</u>.

Being a **Host City** has its **Good** and **Bad** Points

The Olympics are always hosted by a <u>city</u>, not a whole country. <u>Hosting</u> the Games should bring only <u>advantages</u> — but it doesn't always work out like that...

ADVANTAGES

1) The host city gets added <u>prestige</u> — useful if you want to attract <u>trade</u> and <u>tourism</u>.
2) The <u>facilities</u> built for the Games can be used by the locals after the events have finished.
3) <u>Businesses</u> in the host city will do masses of extra trade during the Games.
4) The organisers can try to make a <u>profit</u>.

DISADVANTAGES

1) It's getting more <u>expensive</u> to host the Games every time.
2) If there are problems, the organisers could <u>lose</u> enormous amounts of <u>money</u>.
3) <u>Security</u> could be a problem — <u>hooligans</u> or <u>terrorists</u> might disrupt the Games.
4) If a city's <u>infrastructure</u> (e.g. its phone or transport systems) <u>can't cope</u>, it could lead to <u>frustration</u> for locals and visitors.

> The <u>first ever</u> Olympic Games were held in 776 BC in <u>Ancient Greece</u>.

The **Olympic Games** have had Their **Ups and Downs**

Since the Modern Olympics started in 1896, there have been quite a few ups and downs.

1896 IN ATHENS

The first <u>Modern Olympic Games</u> were organised by <u>Baron de Coubertin</u>. Only men could compete. (See page 88.)

1936 IN BERLIN

<u>Hitler</u> wanted the Games to prove the <u>superiority</u> of <u>white northern Europeans</u>. He stormed out of the stadium when the black American, <u>Jesse Owens</u>, won <u>four gold medals</u>.

1972 IN MUNICH

<u>Palestinian terrorists</u> kidnapped nine Israeli athletes. The hostages, five terrorists and a policeman were <u>killed</u> after a rescue attempt failed.

1980 IN MOSCOW

The USA and many other countries <u>boycotted</u> the Games (i.e. they didn't go to them) as a protest against the Soviet invasion of <u>Afghanistan</u>.

1984 IN LOS ANGELES

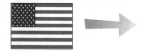

The Games made a big <u>profit</u>, but were thought to be <u>too commercial</u> — nearly everything was <u>sponsored</u> by multinational companies. The USSR <u>boycotted</u> these Games in retaliation for the American boycott in 1980.

1992 IN BARCELONA

<u>No boycotts</u>, and <u>South Africa</u> entered a team for the first time since 1964, when it was <u>banned</u> because of its racist apartheid laws.

Aren't the Olympics great — well done those Ancient Greeks...

The history of the Olympics is important. You might be asked whether you think the 'Olympic Spirit' is still the same as it was originally — you'll need to back up your opinion with facts. Don't worry, the pros and cons above are similar to those on page 104 about international competitions.

Warm-Up and Worked Exam Questions

Warm-up Questions

1) How do small sports clubs cover their costs?
2) Is sponsorship good for a sport, bad for a sport, or a bit of both?
3) Media coverage only does a sport good. True or false?
4) What is the main difference between an amateur and a professional?
5) Which countries tend to train children for a sport from an early age?
6) List two problems that a city might have to deal with when hosting the Olympics.

Worked Exam Questions

Here are the last lot of worked examples and exam questions for you to do. Then it's just the revision summary to have a go at, and you'll be ready to try a lovely practice exam. Lucky you.

1   Jenny plays rugby at a high level. A big drinks company sponsors her.

a) What does this company gain from sponsoring her?

Advertising. Good for the company's image.

(2 marks)

b) List three benefits that Jenny gets from being sponsored. Are there any disadvantages?

Financial help with things like travel, accommodation, equipment.

Free clothing / shoes. Training may be paid for. However, if Jenny

gets injured or performs badly, the sponsor could pull out. They may

try to dictate which events she competes in and abuse their power.

You can treat this as an 'advantages and disadvantages' question.
Just make sure you give the three benefits the question asks for.   *(4 marks)*

2   Janice swims for fun in her spare time, occasionally taking part in competitions. ← Read this bit really carefully first — what is it telling you about Janice's level of participation?

a) What type of athlete is she?

An amateur

(1 mark)

b) Could Janice have taken part in the Olympics in 1896? Explain your answer.

No. Only men were allowed to compete in the first

Olympics in 1896.

(2 marks)

Exam Questions

1   The Olympic Games have often been affected by political events and other problems.

   a)   Explain why some countries boycotted the games in the 1980s.

   ....

   ....

   (2 marks)

   b)   Los Angeles benefited greatly from hosting the games in 1984.
        List two benefits of hosting an international event like the Olympics.

   ....

   ....

   (2 marks)

2   Jack has just watched his favourite team play football on television.

   a)   Name three other forms of media coverage that Jack could use to follow his team.

   ....

   ....

   ....

   (3 marks)

   b)   The club that Jack supports is losing money because of the media coverage it
        receives. Explain why this might be happening.

   ....

   ....

   (2 marks)

3   Chris competes regularly for his local hockey club.

   a)   How do small clubs usually cover the cost of hiring pitches?

   ....

   ....

   (2 marks)

   b)   Chris is an amateur hockey player. Suggest ways in which Chris could get the
        money to train full-time, without being classed as a professional.

   ....

   ....

   ....

   (3 marks)

Revision Summary for Section Four

Well, that's your lot — the final section out of the way. All you have to do now is to make sure you know it all. There are quite a lot of questions here — but like before, I wouldn't try to do them all at once. Just take it easy at first, and you'll be storming through the lot in no time. Enjoy...

1) What's the difference between leisure time and recreation?
2) Give examples of some physical, mental and social benefits of physical recreation.
3) What's the difference between sport and physical recreation?
4) Give four reasons why people generally have more leisure time now than they did 50 years ago.
5) Give three examples of how somebody's family can affect their participation in sport.
6) What is peer pressure? How can it influence somebody's participation in sport?
7) Explain how schools can have an important influence on people's attitudes towards sport.
8) Name nine factors that can affect which sports someone takes part in.
9) Give four reasons why women used to be discouraged from participating in sport.
10) What problems does women's sport still face today? How does the Women's Sports Foundation aim to help solve these problems?
11) What is etiquette? Give two examples of etiquette in sport. What is gamesmanship?
12) Give two ways spectators can help a sports club. What disadvantages could there be in allowing spectators to watch a sporting event?
13) Describe six recommendations made by the Taylor Report after the Heysel and Hillsborough disasters.
14) Draw a diagram to show the structure of a typical local sports club. What are the duties of the chairperson, vice-chairperson, treasurer, secretary, fixtures secretary and membership secretary?
15) Give four functions of a local sports club.
16) Describe 3 ways competitions can be organised, and give advantages and disadvantages for each.
17) Give two examples of outdoor sporting facilities and two examples of indoor facilities.
18) What kinds of things should be considered when planning a new sporting facility?
19) Describe the main differences between public sports facilities and private sports facilities.
20) What are the centres of excellence? Give a couple of examples.
21) Describe four main roles of a national sporting governing body.
22) Give four aims of UK Sport, four sporting aims of the Home Country Councils, and four aims of the CCPR. How is the CCPR funded?
23) Describe the roles of the IOC, the BOA, the SAF, the CC and Sports Coach UK. What do all those initials stand for?
24) Give five possible sources of funding for small clubs and recreational sports facilities.
25) Give two big sources of funding for important clubs playing popular sports.
26) How can companies benefit from sponsoring sports events or individual competitors? Give three examples of the negative side of sponsorship.
27) Describe five positive and five negative effects that the media can have on sport.
28) What's the difference between an amateur and a professional? How did this difference come about?
29) Describe seven ways a competitor could get paid for competing but remain classed as an amateur.
30) Give four examples of big international sporting events. Describe three benefits and three disadvantages to hosting big international sporting competitions.
31) Describe very briefly the different attitudes to sport in: a) the UK, b) the USA, c) the former Eastern Bloc, and d) the Third World.
32) Give four benefits and four drawbacks to hosting the Olympic Games.
33) When were the first Modern Olympics held? Who organised them? Describe the events which blemished the Games in: a) Berlin in 1936, b) Munich in 1972, and c) Moscow in 1980.

Practice Exam

Once you've been through all the questions in this book, you should feel pretty confident about the exam. As final preparation, here is a **practice exam** to really get you set for the real thing. The paper is designed to give you the best possible preparation for the differing question styles of the actual exams, whichever syllabus you're following.

If you're doing **GCSE PE (games)**, you can still use this exam — just answer each question in relation to games, making sure you don't refer to any other physical activities.

General Certificate of Secondary Education

GCSE Physical Education

Centre name				
Centre number				
Candidate number				

Surname	
Other names	
Candidate signature	

Time allowed:
1 hour 45 minutes

Instructions to candidates
- Write your name and other details in the spaces provided above.
- Answer **all** questions in the spaces provided.
- Do all rough work on the paper.

Information for candidates
- The marks available are given in brackets at the end of each question or part-question.
- Marks will not be deducted for incorrect answers.
- There are **2** questions in **Section A** of this paper.
  There are **13** questions in **Section B** of this paper.
  There are **4** questions in **Section C** of this paper.
- There are no blank pages.

Advice to candidates
- Work steadily through the paper.
- Don't spend too long on one question.
- If you have time at the end, go back and check your answers.

SECTION A

Answer ALL questions.

For each part of question 1, choose an answer A, B, C or D and put a cross in the box. Mark only one answer for each question. If you change your mind about an answer, put a line through the box and then mark your new answer with a cross.

eg: Mark the box like this:

    ☒ **A**

    ☒ **B**

    ☒ **C**   *This shows your answer*

    ☒ **D**

If you change your mind, mark the boxes like this:

    ☒ **A**   *This shows your final answer*

    ☒ **B**

    ☒ **C**   *First answer*

    ☒ **D**

1   (a) Obese is:

    ☒ **A** Having an excess of muscle which restricts mobility.

    ☒ **B** The percentage of body weight which is fat, muscle and bone.

    ☒ **C** Muscles in a state of slight tension.

    ☒ **D** Being very overfat.

    (1)

(b) Athlete's foot is caused by:

    ☒ **A** An increase in foot size due to training.

    ☒ **B** A virus.

    ☒ **C** A fungus.

    ☒ **D** An injury associated with 100 m runners.

    (1)

(c) What type of joint is formed by the **atlas and axis** at the neck?

    ☒ **A** Hinge

    ☒ **B** Ball and socket

    ☒ **C** Ball

    ☒ **D** Pivot

    (1)

Edexcel, 2004

Question 2 should be answered by writing **A, B, C** or **D** in the spaces provided.

2 (a) Fitness is:

A a capability of the heart, blood vessels, lungs and muscles to function at optimal efficiency

B the ability to meet the demands of the environment.

C training regularly

D a state of complete mental, physical and social well-being, and not merely the absence of disease and infirmity.

....

(1)

(b) Which of the following statements is **correct** for **all** arteries?

A Take blood away from the heart

B Take blood towards the heart

C Carry oxygenated blood

D Carry deoxygenated blood

....

(1)

(c) Which of the following terms is the correct muscle type for the biceps?

A Voluntary

B Fast twitch

C Slow twitch

D Involuntary

....

(1)

Edexcel, 2003

SECTION B

Answer ALL questions.

3 Why is muscular endurance useful when participating in some physical activities?

....

.... **(1)**

OCR, 2004

4 What is meant by the term 'leisure time'?

....

.... **(1)**

OCR, 2004

5 Explain **one** way in which smoking can reduce performance in a physical activity.

....

....

.... **(1)**

OCR, 2003

6 Explain how the Sit Up test can be used to measure local muscular endurance improvement in a performer.

....

....

....

.... **(2)**

OCR, 2004

7 Explain, using an example, how a synergist muscle works to enable certain movements to take place during a named physical activity.

Physical activity: ....

....

....

....

.... **(2)**

OCR, 2003

8 Identify **two** components of a balanced diet and explain the importance of each component to the performer.

....

....

....

.... **(2)**

OCR, 2003

9 Identify **three** different ways that the production of lactic acid can affect a performer.

....

....

....

....

....

.... **(3)**

OCR, 2004

10 Identify **two** potential hazards a performer may come across when participating in physical activity in the school sports hall and explain how each may affect performance.

Hazard 1: ....

Effect: ....

....

Hazard 2: ....

Effect: ....

....

.... **(4)**

OCR, 2004

11 (a) Complete the table below by ticking the training methods that you think would be **most** likely to increase the aerobic and anaerobic fitness of an athlete. You **may** tick more than one training method for each aspect of fitness.

	Interval	Circuit	Weight
Example: Strength			✓
Aerobic fitness			
Anaerobic fitness			

(4)

(b) What **extreme body type** (somatotype) is associated with elite athletes who carry out a lot of

   (i) strength training ....

(1)

   (ii) continuous training ....

(1)

(Total 6 marks)

Edexcel, 2004

12 Air contains Oxygen, Carbon Dioxide and Nitrogen.

(a) What is the percentage of oxygen in inspired air?

....

(1)

(b) How do the ribs and diaphragm move to aid inspiration?

Ribs: ....

Diaphragm: ....

(2)

(c) What is the percentage of oxygen in expired air?

....

(1)

(d) Why is there a difference between the amount of oxygen inspired and expired?

....

....

(1)

(e) What happens to the levels of carbon dioxide and nitrogen in expired air?

Carbon Dioxide levels: ....

Explanation: ....

....

(2)

Nitrogen levels: ....

Explanation: ....

....

(2)

(Total 9 marks)

Edexcel, 2003

13 Referees and umpires help prevent injury to players by enforcing the rules of an activity.

(a) The chances of becoming injured are also reduced by **balancing competition**. Explain the term 'balancing competition'.

....

(1)

(b) State **FOUR** ways that competition in activities could be balanced.

1. ....

(1)

2. ....

(1)

3. ....

(1)

4. ....

(1)

(c) Name an activity of your choice, giving specific examples of **TWO** ways in which competition within that activity is balanced.

ACTIVITY ....

1. ....

(1)

2. ....

(1)

(d) State **THREE** other ways (apart from obeying the rules and balancing competition), that performers can reduce the risk of injury.

1. ....

(1)

2. ....

(1)

3. ....

(1)

(Total 10 marks)

Edexcel, 2004

14 **Figure 1** shows the legs of a runner.

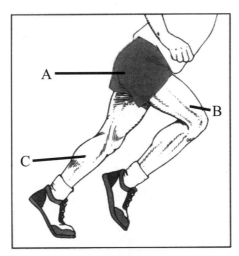

Figure 1

(a) Label the muscles **A**, **B** and **C**.

(i) **A** ....

(i) **B** ....

(iii) **C** ....

(3)

(b) Which muscle, **A**, **B** or **C**, allows the runner to drive forwards off the toes during his running action?

....

(1)

(c) Which muscle, **A**, **B** or **C**, allows the runner to extend the leg at the hip?

....

(1)

(d) Two of the muscles named in the box below work as an **antagonistic pair**. Name the two muscles.

Bicep	Deltoid	Gluteals
Hamstrings		Quadriceps

.... and ....

(1)

(e) Explain the term 'antagonistic pair'.

....

....

(1)

(Total 7 marks)

Edexcel, 2004

15 The cardiovascular and respiratory systems make up the cardio-respiratory system.

(a) What are the **three** components of the cardiovascular system?

....
(1)

(b) What are the **two** components of the respiratory system?

....
(1)

(c) State **one** reason why it is important for a performer to improve their cardiovascular systems.

....
(1)

(d) Complete the table below by stating the **anatomical** names of the labelled parts in Figure 2 and explain their function.

Figure 2 is a diagram of the heart.

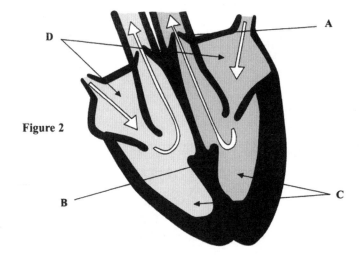

Figure 2

Label	Anatomical Name	Function
A		
B		
C		
D		

(8)

(e) (i) What happens to an individual's **heart rate** when they start exercising?

....

....

(1)

(ii) Why is this an advantage to the performer?

....

....

(1)

(f) (i) Define **cardiac output** and state how it is affected when an individual starts to exercise.

Cardiac output: ....

Effect of exercise on cardiac output: ....

....

(2)

(ii) How does the heart achieve this change in cardiac output?

....

....

(1)

(Total 16 marks)
Edexcel, 2003

SECTION C

Answer ALL questions.

16 (a) (i) What are the **two** main benefits to fitness which can be achieved by the use of weight training?

Benefit 1 ....

Benefit 2 ....

(2)

(ii) In relation to weight training, what is meant by the following?

Repetitions ....

....

Sets ....

....

....

(2)

(iii) Explain what it meant by the term "reversibility" in relation to weight training.

....

....

....

....

....

(2)

(b) Flexibility is an important component of fitness.

(i) Briefly describe a test which can be used to measure flexibility.

....

....

....

....

....

(2)

(ii) How can flexibility be improved?

....

....

....

....

....

(2)

(c) Some performers may take banned drugs such as anabolic steroids to enhance their performance.

(i) Name **two** other **types** of banned drug which performers may use to improve their performance.

Type 1 ....

Type 2 ....

(2)

(ii) **Explain** why performers might be tempted to use anabolic steroids and **describe** the effects they can have.

....

....

....

....

....

....

....

(3)
(Total 15 marks)
AQA, 2004

17 (a) The media can have a great influence on the levels of participation in sport.

(i) **Name three** different forms of the media.

1. ....

2. ....

3. ....

(3)

(ii) **Describe two** ways in which the media can help to give a greater understanding of performance.

1. ....

....

....

2. ....

....

....

(2)

(iii) **Describe two** ways in which media coverage may have affected sport.

1. ....

....

....

2. ....

....

....

(2)

(b) Correct etiquette is expected in sports activities.

    (i) What is meant by etiquette?

....

....

....

(2)

    (ii) Give **two** examples of correct sporting etiquette.

1. ....

....

....

2. ....

....

....

(2)

(c) Sport is often considered to be either professional or amateur.

    (i) What is meant by an amateur sports person?

....

....

....

....

(2)

    (ii) What is meant by a professional sports person?

....

....

....

....

(2)

(d) Sponsorship is very common in sport.

(i) Briefly describe **three** different ways in which sponsorship can be provided for a **sports performer**.

1. ....

....

....

2. ....

....

....

3. ....

....

....

(3)

(ii) Describe a form of sponsorship which might **not** be considered to be acceptable in sport, clearly stating why.

....

....

....

....

....

(2)

(Total 20 marks)

AQA, 2003

18 Fara is a 100m hurdler. She trains regularly and thinks carefully about her Personal
    Exercise Programme (PEP) as she has seen many of her team mates injured through over
    training. To help her understand the requirements of her sport, she analyses her
    performance regularly. Fara's coach told her that her training was proving effective as her
    performance was improving.

    (a) Define the term 'performance'.

    ....
                                                                                                    (1)

    (b) The following are statements taken from Fara's PEP.

    A I need to make sure my training matches the requirement of my sport, therefore
         I shall be using interval training.

    B I found the workload far too easy last week so I shall be training harder this
         week.

    C I think it is important to gradually increase the amount of work that I do.

    D I need to structure my PEP to my needs, no one else's.

    E Unfortunately I had to have a minor operation on my knee. I was unable to train
         for 6 weeks, which means that I have already started to lose my fitness.

    (i) Complete the table below by naming **THREE** principles of training (other than
         the F.I.T.T. principle) that Fara has referred to in the statements from her PEP.
         Explain the meaning of each of the principles.

	Principles of training	Explanation
1		
2		
3		

                                                                                                    (6)

(ii) Complete the table below to match each of the statements from Fara's PEP to the correct principle of training.

Statement from PEP	Principle of Training
A	
C	
E	

(3)

(c) During a recent competition one of the hurdlers fell and sprained her ankle.

(i) State **ONE visible** symptom of a sprained ankle.

....
(1)

(ii) What type of injury is a sprained ankle?

....
(1)

(iii) What treatment should she be given for this type of injury?

....
(1)

(d) **Figure 3** shows a diagram of the skeleton of the lower leg and foot.

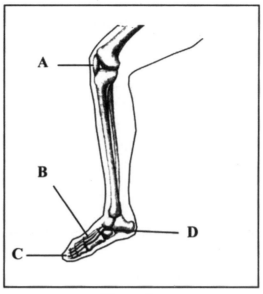

Figure 3

(i) Name the bones labelled **A**, **B**, **C** and **D**.

A ....
(1)

B ....
(1)

C ....
(1)

D ....
(1)

(ii) The bones labelled **D** are short bones. How does the function of a short bone help the hurdler?

....
(1)

(e) The 100m hurdles is a sprint event.

(i) What type of muscle fibres would be most useful to a 100m hurdler?

Fibre type ....
(1)

(ii) Why would this type of muscle fibre be useful to a 100m hurdler?

....
(1)

(Total 20 marks)

Edexcel, 2004

19   International performers who participate in major events and competitions, such as the Commonwealth Games, are top level performers. They will often have started learning skills from an early age. In order to compete at such high levels, they also need to be highly motivated and have an efficient muscular system.

(a)   Identify **one** reason why an efficient muscular system is important to a top level performer.

....

....
                                                                                                            (1)

(b)   Briefly explain how antagonistic muscles produce efficient movement.

....

....

....

....
                                                                                                            (2)

(c)   Identify **three** social factors that could encourage participation in physical activity from an early age.

....

....

....

....

....
                                                                                                            (3)

(d) Major international events can help encourage participation in physical activity at a local level. Identify **three** possible reasons for this.

....

....

....

....

....

(3)

(e) Describe how politics and tradition can positively affect top level participation in physical activity.

....

....

....

....

....

....

(4)

(f) Intrinsic and extrinsic motivation are important to all top level performers. Explain the meaning of each and why intrinsic motivation is the more important.

....

....

....

....

....

....

(4)

(g) Using examples, explain why the skills of a novice performer will differ from those of a top level performer.

....

....

....

....

....

....

....

....

....

....

....

....

....

....

....

(8)
(Total 25 marks)
OCR, 2004

END

Section One — The Human Body

Page 6 (Warm-Up Questions)

1) 206
2) vital organs
3) femur
4) cartilage
5) extension
6) tendons, ligaments, cartilage

Page 7 (Exam Questions)

1   A — cranium

     B — scapula

     C — femur

     D — clavicle

     E — tibia

     You need to check very carefully where exactly each arrow is pointing to.

2   bone marrow

3   (1 mark for each correct function.)

Connective Tissue	Function
Cartilage	Absorb impacts / protect the ends of the bones
Ligaments	Connect bones to other bones
Tendons	Connect muscles to bones

4) a) ball and socket

    b) hip

    c) flexion, extension, *(1 mark)* adduction, abduction *(1 mark)*

Page 12 (Warm-Up Questions)

1) pull
2) an antagonistic pair
3) speed
4) voluntary, involuntary, cardiac
5) isotonic

Page 13 (Exam Questions)

1   a) A — trapezius

       B — triceps

       C — latissimus dorsi

       D — gluteals/gluteus maximus

       E — hamstring

       F — gastrocnemius

    b) Origin is the place where the muscle is attached to the stationary bone/the bone that doesn't move *(1 mark)*. The insertion is the place where the muscle is attached to the moving bone *(1 mark)*.

2   When flexing the knee, the hamstring *(1 mark)* is the prime mover/agonist and the quadriceps *(1 mark)* is the antagonist *(1 mark)*.

     Don't just say "hamstring and quadriceps" — you need to say which is the agonist and which is the antagonist if you want to get all the marks.

3

Condition	Definition	Cause
Muscle fatigue	tired, weak muscles	overuse / lack of oxygen
Muscle atrophy	muscles get smaller	muscles not used enough
Cramp	sudden contraction of a muscle, which then won't relax	lack of salts / lack of blood flow to muscle

(1 mark for each correct line of the table)

Page 16 (Warm-Up Questions)

1) oxygen
2) red blood cells
3) oxygen and carbon dioxide
4) The maximum volume of oxygen used by your body in one minute.
5) the alveoli (in the lungs)
6) It gets faster

Page 17 (Exam Questions)

1   a) A — nasal cavity/nose

       B — trachea/windpipe

       C — bronchus/bronchi

       D — bronchioles

       E — alveoli

    b) Oxygen diffuses from the air in the alveoli into the blood *(1 mark)*. Carbon dioxide diffuses out of the blood into the air in the alveoli *(1 mark)*.

       Don't forget that gas exchange occurs in both directions.

2   6 — air is forced out of the lungs

     1 — the intercostal muscles and the diaphragm contract

     3 — a pressure difference draws air into the lungs

     4 — the intercostal muscles and diaphragm relax

     2 — the chest cavity becomes larger

     5 — the chest cavity becomes smaller.

     (4 marks if all correct. Deduct 1 mark for each number incorrect.)

     With this kind of question, it's a good idea to try to visualise what's happening. Try to remember those breathing diagrams on page 15.

3   a) Tidal volume — the amount you breathe in (or out) with each breath *(1 mark)*.

       Vital capacity — the most air you could possibly breathe in (or out) in one breath *(1 mark)*.

    b) You breathe quicker and deeper *(1 mark)*, so oxygen uptake increases *(1 mark)*.

     This is a two mark question, so you need to say more than just "it increases".

Page 21 (Warm-Up Questions)

1) improving muscle size
2) two
3) deoxygenated blood
4) arteries
5) red blood cells
6) white blood cells

Page 22 (Exam Questions)

1

Part	Name	Function
A	(tricuspid) valve	prevents backflow of blood into the atrium
B	pulmonary artery	takes deoxygenated blood to the lungs
C	aorta	takes blood to the body
D	pulmonary vein	brings oxygenated blood back from the lungs

It's not enough to just know the labels — you've got to learn what each bit does. That means making sure you really understand the diagram.

2   a) Age, gender, exercise, stress

     (1 mark for each correct factor, up to a maximum of 3)

b)

Type of blood vessel	Function	Thickness of walls
Arteries	Carry oxygenated blood away from the heart	Thick
Veins	Carry deoxygenated blood back to the heart	Thinner
Capillaries	Carry blood directly to and from tissues	Very thin

Use the information already in the table to work out what kind of answer you need to write in the spaces.

3 a) red blood cells

b) white blood cells

c) platelets

d) plasma

Section Two — Health and Fitness

Page 27 (Warm-Up Questions)

1) good reactions

2) tobacco and alcohol

3) General fitness is the ability to cope with everyday life / the demands of your environment. Specific fitness is about having specific abilities needed for a sport, e.g. speed for sprinting.

4) Cardiovascular fitness is the ability of your heart and lungs to keep your body supplied with oxygen. Muscular fitness is the ability of your muscles to produce a lot of force.

5) Speed, strength, stamina and suppleness.

6) Level of exercise a person needs depends on their level of fitness, weight, age and gender. It also depends on their goals and the fitness requirements of the activities they do.

Page 28 (Exam Questions)

1 a) They smoke / drink too much alcohol, they have a bad diet, they are unhygienic / smell, they are always stressed / anxious or suffer from a mental illness *(1 mark each for any two reasons)*.

b) E.g. netball. Physical benefit — get fitter by training regularly. Mental benefit — relieve stress and have fun. Social benefit — make new friends within team *(1 mark for each type of benefit)*.

2

Sport	Fitness component	Used for
Football	Agility	Turning quickly on the ball
Tennis	Coordination	Striking the ball accurately
Basketball	Power / explosive strength	To jump high for rebounds
Marathon	Stamina / CV Endurance	To keep going the whole distance
Sprinter	Fast reactions	Starting

3 a) Cardiovascular fitness is the body's ability to keep going for a long time / the efficiency of the heart and lungs in delivering oxygen to the working muscles.

It's really important that you learn ALL the definitions — otherwise you'll be throwing away easy marks in the exam.

b) Regular exercise that involves the heart and lungs being used a lot, e.g., running. Not smoking.

c) Muscular fitness would be most important to a weightlifter *(1 mark)* because weightlifting involves applying maximum force / power over a short period of time *(1 mark)*.

Page 32 (Warm-Up Questions)

1) It goes up

2) It gets faster and deeper

3) The fitter you are, the faster you recover.

4) Aerobic exercise means working over a long duration, maintaining a high breathing and heart rate.

5) A short-term effect disappears soon after you stop exercising. A long-term effect is a more permanent change.

6) Muscles become thicker and can contract more strongly. Tendons become bigger and stronger.

Page 33 (Exam Questions)

1 Paddy is fitter. The graph shows that Dee's heart rate goes up higher *(1 mark)* and quicker *(1 mark)* than Paddy's. Paddy's resting heart rate is lower *(1 mark)*. Paddy's heart rate returns to pre-exercise levels much quicker *(1 mark)*.

This is a big four mark question, so you need to go into plenty of detail about what the graph tells you about the students' fitness.

2 a) Stronger respiratory muscles, increased vital capacity, increased capillarisation around alveoli, gaseous exchange speeds up *(1 mark each for any three points)*.

b) To keep taking in high amounts of oxygen in order to repay the oxygen debt *(1 mark)*, and to remove waste products such as lactic acid *(1 mark)*.

Page 39 (Warm-Up Questions)

1) Being very overweight — having at least 20% more body fat than is normal for your height and build.

2) Carbohydrates

3) Oranges (or any citrus fruit)

4) Exercise

5) Heart and lungs

6) Aerobic: Glucose + oxygen → Carbon Dioxide + Water + Energy

Anaerobic: Glucose → Lactic Acid + Energy

Page 40 (Exam Questions)

1 a) Chris should eat a lot of protein to build/repair his muscles *(1 mark)*. Val should eat a lot of carbohydrates to provide energy *(1 mark)*.

b) Val's body converts glucose into energy using aerobic respiration *(1 mark)*. This requires her muscles to be well supplied with oxygen *(1 mark)*.

Glucose + Oxygen → Energy + Carbon Dioxide + Water *(1 mark)*

Make sure you know the two equations for respiration. And don't get them confused.

2 a) It is the energy needed to keep the heart beating, the body breathing, and all the other processes that occur when the body is at rest happening.

b) Amount of exercise, age, lifestyle, gender. *(Any 3 factors, maximum 3 marks)*

3 a) Lactic acid

b) Lactic acid is produced when there is a lack of oxygen. Its build-up causes fatigue and pain in muscles.

Page 47 (Warm-Up Questions)

1) fast-twitch

2) strength and speed

3) static, explosive and dynamic

4) oxygen capacity, reaction times, flexibility

5) body shape

6) e.g., snooker, golf, archery

Page 48 (Exam Questions)

1

Fitness Component	Sport	Why component is needed
Strength	Rugby	To push in scrum/hand-off
Power	Tennis	To serve and smash
Speed	Sprinting	To win the race
Flexibility	Gymnastics	To get into different positions

2   In general: men have longer / heavier bones, men have more muscle, women have more body fat, women physically mature earlier, menstruation can affect performance. *(Any 3 physical factors, maximum 3 marks)*

3   a) Endomorph — wide hips, narrow shoulders, lots of body fat, relatively thin wrists and ankles *(1 mark)*.
Ectomorph — narrow shoulders, hips and chest, little muscle or fat, long thin limbs and face *(1 mark)*.
Mesomorph — wide shoulders, relatively narrow hips, muscular, strong arms and legs, little body fat *(1 mark)*.
You don't need all these details to get the marks — two key features of each somatotype will do.

b) Endomorph — e.g. sumo wrestling, shot-put *(1 mark)*.
Ectomorph — e.g. basketball, high jump, long-distance running *(1 mark)*.
Mesomorph — e.g. swimming, gymnastics, decathlon *(1 mark)*.

Page 54 (Warm-Up Questions)

1) Wash regularly, clean your teeth, change your clothes regularly.

2) Wash and dry feet properly, wear clean socks, wear flip-flops in shared changing areas, avoid shoes and socks that make feet sweat a lot.

3) Improve performance / calm nerves

4) Using urine samples.

5) Illness or medical condition, staleness, fatigue, lack of sleep, menstruation.

6) Psychological factors (the state your mind is in)

Page 55 (Exam Questions)

1   a) A viral infection resulting in a flat wart that grows on the bottom of your feet.

b) Avoided by wearing flip-flops or similar footwear in shared changing areas. Treated with ointments / pads.

2   a)

Name of Drug	Effect on Performance	Side Effects
Anabolic Steroids	ability to train longer, increased muscle size	high blood pressure, heart disease, infertility, cancer
Stimulants	speed up reactions, increase aggression	high blood pressure, heart and liver problems, strokes
Narcotic Analgesics	kill pain	constipation, low blood pressure
EPO (polypeptide hormones)	increase muscle size, ability to train harder	strokes, abnormal growth
Diuretics	weight loss caused by frequent urination	cramp, dehydration
Beta blockers	lower heart rate, reduce anxiety	addiction

(1 mark for each correct entry, plus 1 extra mark if all correct)

To get the marks, you only really need one effect and one side effect for each drug. If you think you know more than one though, it doesn't hurt to write them both down — one of them might not be as right as you think.

b) Blood is taken from the athlete (red blood cells separated) *(1 mark)*. The body produces more red blood cells to replace the lost ones *(1 mark)*. The red blood cells from the removed blood are then reinjected before a competition *(1 mark)*, giving the athlete a greater number of red blood cells and improving oxygen transport *(1 mark)*.

3   For example, football needs agility to turn quickly on the ball, balance so you don't fall over and coordination so you make contact with the ball *(1 mark each for any three suitable points)*.
Use a sport you know well so you can be as specific as possible in your answer.

Section Three — Training & Sporting Skills

Page 60 (Warm-Up Questions)

1) cool-down

2) Specificity, Progression, Overload, Reversibility

3) do a variety of things in each session, do some cross training

4) out-of-season preparation, pre-season preparation, competition, recuperation

5) at least 20 minutes twice a week

6) Doing an exercise that's not directly relevant to your sport — increases fitness, but does not strain the same muscles and joints as your main activity.

Page 61 (Exam Questions)

1   a) It is likely to have decreased.

b) reversibility

c) Specificity — this is training the right body parts for your sport *(1 mark)*.
Progression — steadily increasing the amount of training *(1 mark)*.
Overload — making your body work hard enough to make it fitter *(1 mark)*.
Remember your SPOR principles of training.

2   a) Janice could include different activities in her training sessions such as cycling or swimming. She could enter smaller competitions to check and assess her training.
There are two marks available, so try to come up with two suggestions.

b) A cool-down pays off the oxygen debt and gets rid of lactic acid in the muscles. It prevents blood pooling and gets rid of any extra blood in the muscles *(1 mark each for any two suitable points)*.

3   He could do some out-of-season preparation, consisting of lots of aerobic and strength training *(1 mark)*, some pre-season preparation, including aerobic, anaerobic and skills training *(1 mark)*. He could compete regularly during the competition season *(1 mark)*, and recuperate afterwards *(1 mark)*.

Page 65 (Warm-Up Questions)

1) A sprinter leaving the starting blocks.

2) Isometric

3) No, because no movement is produced.

4) It involves changes of speed and exercise type without stopping in between.

5) It can be boring / it doesn't improve sprinting.

6) Interval training

Page 66 (Exam Questions)

1   a) Continuous training, as it has no rest periods and is most like cross-country. (Fartlek training would also be okay here.)

b) It can be really boring.

c) By increasing the duration, distance, speed or frequency of training.
(1 mark each for any two suggestions)

2   a) Pressure training.

b) It can be less enjoyable *(1 mark)* and it is not relevant for amateurs *(1 mark)*.

3   a) Circuit training / fartlek training

b) She should work for at least an hour *(1 mark)* at 60-90% of her VO_2 max *(1 mark)*.

c) It does not improve sprinting, which she needs in her hockey playing.

Page 69 (Warm-Up Questions)

1) A dynamometer

2) The carotid artery (neck) or the radial artery (wrist).

3) The Stork Stand Test

4) Maximal Oxygen Consumption — the maximum volume of oxygen your body can use in a minute.

If you've forgotten what Maximal Oxygen Consumption (VO_2 max) actually is, look back at page 15 for an explanation.

Page 69 (Exam Questions)

1 a) Balance, flexibility, strength and agility *(1 mark each for any two)*.

   b) *For example:*

     Balance — The Stork Stand Test *(1 mark)*, stand on one leg with your other foot touching your knee, your hands on your hips, and your eyes closed *(1 mark)*. Time how long you can stand like that without moving your feet or your hands, or opening your eyes *(1 mark)*.

     Remember to say what measurement is recorded by the tester, as well as what the person being tested needs to do.

2 a) Lower heart rate at rest and whilst exercising *(1 mark)*/ can exercise for longer without feeling tired *(1 mark)* / can use up more oxygen when exercising *(1 mark)*.

   b) Harvard Step Test, 12-minute run, Multistage Fitness Test *(1 mark each for any two)*

   c) The Harvard Step Test — You need a 45 cm step. The participant must complete 30 step-ups a minute for 5 minutes *(1 mark)*. Rest for a minute then measure your pulse rate. Use the formula to calculate your score *(1 mark)*.

     The 12-minute run — Run around a track as many times as you can for 12 minutes *(1 mark)*. Record the distance run *(1 mark)*.

     The Multistage Fitness Test — You need two lines 20 metres apart. Use a recording of bleeps to run timed shuttles between the two lines. The time between the bleeps gets shorter so you have to run faster. If you miss 3 bleeps, you must stop *(1 mark)*. Record the level and number of shuttles completed to get a score for the test *(1 mark)*.

Page 76 (Warm-Up Questions)

1) Making sure all competitors are of a similar size, strength and skill level.

2) Hard-tissue injuries are when the bone is damaged. Anything else is a soft-tissue injury.

3) Rest, Ice, Compression and Elevation.

4) Give them mouth-to-mouth ventilation until breathing starts, then place them in the recovery position.

5) Shin splints / tennis elbow / golfer's elbow

6) In an open injury the skin is broken, in a closed one the injury is internal.

Page 77 (Exam Questions)

1 a) Hypothermia — rigid muscles, irregular heartbeat, may be unconscious.

   b) They would need to steadily raise the body temperature to 37 °C *(1 mark)*. They could give extra clothing or a blanket / sleeping bag to the sufferer *(1 mark)*. They could also give them a hot drink *(1 mark)*.

   c) Hyperthermia *(1 mark)*. The sufferer has a weak pulse and clammy pale skin *(1 mark)*. Get the patient to lie down in a cool place and give them lots of liquids. Get advice from a doctor if possible *(1 mark)*.

     This question is asking for three things — the name of the condition, the symptoms and the treatment. Make sure you cover all three in your answer.

2 a) A hard-tissue injury / a fracture.

   b) An open fracture *(1 mark)*, which is where the bone pokes through the skin *(1 mark)*, or a closed fracture *(1 mark)*, which occurs under the skin *(1 mark)*.

   c) This is an acute injury because it was caused by falling onto the ground.

Page 78 (Exam Questions)

3 a) A dislocation or torn cartilage.

   b) This is the treatment for cramp *(1 mark)*. Cramp is caused by a lack of mineral salts in the blood *(1 mark)* or a lack of blood flowing to a muscle *(1 mark)*.

   c) It involves mouth-to-mouth ventilation *(1 mark)* and cardiac massage *(1 mark)*.

4 a) She should follow DRABC:

     Danger — make sure that the casualty is safe

     Response — check if they respond to your voice

     Airway — clear the airway (if it isn't already clear)

     Breathing — look for signs of breathing

     Circulation — check if they have a pulse

     Give CPR if necessary

     (1 mark for writing down each step of DRABC, 1 mark for explaining them, 1 mark for CPR)

     Just writing down an acronym like DRABC is never enough — the acronym is just to help you remember the real information, which is what you need to write down.

   b) They may be in shock or have concussion.

   c) Place them in the recovery position and call an ambulance.

Page 82 (Warm-Up Questions)

1) E.g. jumping, running

2) Open

3) Intrinsic and Extrinsic. Intrinsic motivation comes from within, e.g. the satisfaction you get from doing something well. Extrinsic motivation comes from outside, e.g. prizes and other rewards for winning.

4) When the brain filters out all the extra information and only processes the relevant information to perform the skill.

5) Specific, Measurable, Agreed, Realistic, Time-phased, Exciting, Recorded

6) If your arousal level becomes too high you may be 'psyched out' or too 'stressed out' and you will not be able to perform at your best.

Page 83 (Exam Questions)

1 a) It's the urge to do something well for your own satisfaction. It comes from within, and drives you on to succeed.

   b) Extrinsic motivation *(1 mark)*. Intrinsic motivation comes from inside you *(1 mark)*. Extrinsic motivation comes from outside *(1 mark)*. You play well because there is a big reward, e.g. money or a trophy *(1 mark)*.

     Don't just explain what extrinsic motivation is — you need to compare it to intrinsic motivation to get all the marks.

2 a) Dan *(1 mark)*, as his arousal level is just right. He is neither too relaxed or too stressed *(1 mark)*.

   b) It helps you to focus on what you wanted to achieve *(1 mark)*.
It helps you feel in control and so less anxious about the race *(1 mark)*.
Achieving goals increases confidence *(1 mark)*.
It can motivate you to try harder *(1 mark)*.

3 a) A skill is a learned ability *(1 mark)* to bring about the result you want, with maximum certainty and efficiency *(1 mark)*.

   b) It's a mixture of both *(1 mark)*. It can be defined as a closed skill because it is not greatly affected by factors such as the wind *(1 mark)*. However, it can also be defined as an open skill because you can change the speed and aim of the shot in response to the goalkeeper's position or movement *(1 mark)*.

     The fact that the question asks you to explain your answer is a fair indication that the examiner's not going to be impressed with a simple 'yes' or 'no'.

Section Four — Sport in Society
Page 91 (Warm-Up Questions)

1) Free time, when you're not meeting bodily or social needs.

2) Things you do in your leisure time because you want to.

3) The National Curriculum

4) Two from:

     Sports can be considered 'male only'.

     Women are often not allowed to compete with men.

     Poor media coverage (low profile).

     Less sponsorship/prize money

     Few role models for women.

5) Etiquette

6) 1985

Page 92 (Exam Questions)

1 a) Benefits: spectators can be a positive influence on a team by cheering them on and putting off the opposition. They also spend money on tickets and merchandise which brings money into the club. *(2 marks for two benefits fully explained)*

Problems: spectators can cost money — they require facilities, marshalling and policing that have to be paid for by clubs. There is also the potential problem of hooliganism. *(2 marks for two problems fully explained)*

b) Opposing fans should be separated by fences, some stadiums should be all-seater, troublemakers barred from entering grounds, fences between spectators and the pitch should be removed, closed circuit television cameras in stadiums, information on hooligans shared between police forces in different countries. *(1 mark for each recommendation, up to a maximum of 3 marks)*

2 Sport is competitive, has rules, organised events and competitions and the aim is to win *(1 mark)*. Physical recreation isn't competitive. You're not competing against anyone other than yourself so you can set your own rules *(1 mark)*.

3 a) John might have a lot of leisure time because he has taken early retirement. He may also have machines (such as dishwashers, washing machines, etc.) that can do household chores.

b) John's age could mean that he wants to do less strenuous, indoor activities.

c) Any two from:
Money — John may not be able to afford to play a more expensive sport.
Facilities — there may be badminton courts close to where John lives (availability of facilities is linked to politics).
Fashion — badminton may be fashionable at the moment.
Danger — John may dislike more dangerous sports.
(1 mark for each of two factors, 1 mark for each explanation. Maximum of four marks.)
This is a four mark question, but it's only asking for two things. This should set the alarm bells ringing — you're gonna need to explain each of those two points in order to get all the marks. The word 'discuss' should also give you a clue...

Page 97 (Warm-Up Questions)

1) To manage club finances
2) League
3) Outdoor – it's a watersports centre
4) A council or local authority
5) International Olympic Committee
6) UK Sport

Page 98 (Exam Questions)

1 a) The council will need to think about:
Whether people are going to use it.
Whether there will be space to park.
How people will get to it — public transport services?
The cost of the project.
Whether it will have to compete with other facilities in the area.
Whether it can be used for other things.
(1 mark for each consideration, up to a maximum of 4)

b) Local authorities and councils own public sector facilities. They usually run at a loss *(1 mark)*. For example, leisure centres, swimming pools and pitches *(1 mark)*. Private sector facilities are owned by individuals or companies. They aim to make money, or at least break even *(1 mark)*. For example, health clubs, golf clubs *(1 mark)*.

2 a) BOA — the British Olympic Association.

b) The IOC:
Runs the Olympics.
Decides where to hold the games.
Decides which sports to include.
Helps to plan the games.
Fights against doping and corruption.
(1 mark for each role, up to a maximum of 4)

3 a) SAF — Sports Aid Foundation

b) UK Sport

Page 106 (Warm-Up Questions)

1) Membership fees, match fees, gambling levies
2) A bit of both
3) False
4) An amateur does not get paid and a professional does.
5) Former Eastern Bloc countries
6) Games are very expensive to host / threat of terrorism and hooligans / strain on local infrastructure.

Page 107 (Exam Questions)

1 a) 1980 — The USA and other countries boycotted the games as a protest against the invasion of Afghanistan by the Soviet Union *(1 mark)*.
1984 — The USSR boycotted the games in retaliation for the American boycott *(1 mark)*.

b) Hosting the games gains prestige, which attracts tourism and trade. The facilities can be used after the games. Local businesses get extra trade and it can make a profit for the organisers.
(1 mark each for any two of the above)

2 a) Radio, internet, Ceefax or Teletext, newspapers and magazines.
(1 mark each for any three of the above)

b) People are watching the team on the TV rather than attending games *(1 mark)*, so ticket sales are decreasing and merchandise is not being sold at the ground *(1 mark)*.

3 a) They collect membership and match fees *(1 mark)*. They may also run fund-raising activities, e.g. raffles *(1 mark)*.

b) Chris could get a scholarship at a college. He could compete professionally, but put his prize money into a trust fund. He could get sponsored by a company. He could accept large expenses payments, or gifts for competing. He could find a company willing to give him a "token job" that would allow him to train full-time. He could accept payments and keep quiet about it (though this is illegal). *(1 mark per suggestion, up to a maximum of 3)*
Although it doesn't tell you to give a certain number of suggestions, you can tell from the marks available that you should write about three ways that Chris could get to train full-time.

EXAM PAPER ANSWERS

Please note: The answers to the past exam questions have not been provided or approved by the examining bodies (AQA, OCR and London Qualifications Ltd - Edexcel). As such, AQA, OCR and London Qualifications Ltd do not accept any responsibility for the accuracy and method of the working in the answers given. CGP has provided suggested solutions — other possible solutions may be equally correct.

Exam Paper

1 a) D *(1 mark)*
b) C *(1 mark)*
c) D *(1 mark)*

2 a) B *(1 mark)*
b) A *(1 mark)*
c) A *(1 mark)*

3 It allows your muscles to exert force for a long time. This is useful for activities that require power, but not just in a single burst. *(1 mark)*

4 Free time, when you're not meeting bodily or social needs. *(1 mark)*

5 It reduces the efficiency of the lungs / kills cilia.
It increases the risk of heart disease and lung, throat and liver cancer.
Narrows the arteries that lead to the muscles.
It reduces the ability of blood to carry oxygen.
(1 mark for any of the above)

6 Test how many sit ups a performer can do in 30 seconds *(1 mark)*.
Repeat the test every few weeks and compare the results to show changes in muscular endurance *(1 mark)*.

7 Synergists help other muscles / the prime mover function by holding other parts of the body in position while the movement takes place. E.g. abdominal muscles when kicking football *(2 marks)*. *(No marks for just a named activity)*

8 Carbohydrates — provide energy.
Proteins — used for muscular growth and repair.
Water — maintain fluid balance and prevent dehydration.
Fats — warmth, protection of vital organs, reserve fuel supply.
Vitamins — regulate chemical reactions and used for growth and repair.
Minerals — specific roles, e.g., calcium needed for muscle function and strong bones.

(2 marks for any two of the above)

9 Makes muscles feel tired and weak.
Causes muscles to become painful.
Eventually stops muscles from working.

(1 mark each for the three points above)

10 E.g.,
Slippery floors — may make it difficult to change direction quickly. May lead to slipping and injury.
Walls — possibility of colliding with walls may mean that performers have to reduce their speed. Collision may cause impact injuries.
Other performers — If the sports hall is busy, other people's activities may get in the way — risk of injury from being hit with balls etc., or from running into people.

(2 marks for any two hazards. 2 marks for two matching effects.)

11 a)

	Interval	Circuit	Weight
Aerobic fitness	✓	✓	
Anaerobic fitness	✓	✓	✓

(1 mark for each tick correct. Deduct 1 mark for each tick in an incorrect box.)

b) i) Mesomorph *(1 mark)*

ii) Ectomorph *(1 mark)*

12 a) 21% (accept 20% or 22%) *(1 mark)*

b) **Ribs** — move up and out. *(1 mark)*
Diaphragm — moves down / flattens / contracts. *(1 mark)*

c) 16% (accept 15% or 17%) *(1 mark)*

d) Some oxygen has been absorbed / used by the body. *(1 mark)*

e) **Carbon Dioxide levels** — increase. *(1 mark)*
Explanation — it is produced by the body / it is a waste product. *(1 mark)*
Nitrogen levels — stay the same. *(1 mark)*
Explanation — it's not used or created by the body.

13 a) Trying to even out the sides / making competitors compete against competitors of similar ability. *(1 mark)* *(Just writing 'balancing sides' is not acceptable.)*

b) Grade competitors by skill / ability level.
Grade competitors by weight.
Grade competitors by age.
Grade competitors by gender.
(1 mark for each)

c) E.g., Squash — Over 50s play in a separate section of a tournament.
Women and men compete separately.
Boxing — Weight categories imposed on competition.
Women and men compete separately.
(2 marks for two examples of balancing, relevant to stated activity)

d) Protective clothing / correct clothing (including the removal of jewellery).
Protective equipment / correct equipment.
Warm up / make sure you are fit to take part.
Suitable playing area / check playing surface.
(3 marks for any three of the above.) *('Cool down' is not acceptable.)*

14 a) i) A — Gluteals / Gluteus maximus *(1 mark)*
('Glutes' is not acceptable.)

ii) B — Quadriceps *(1 mark)*
('Quads' is not acceptable.)

iii) C — Gastrocnemius *(1 mark)*

b) Gastrocnemius / C *(1 mark)*

c) Gluteals / A *(1 mark)*

d) Hamstrings **and** Quadriceps *(Both muscles needed for 1 mark)*

e) One muscle of the pair contracts, while the other muscle relaxes. They work together in this way to bring about movement.

15 a) Heart, blood and blood vessels.

b) Lungs and breathing.

c) Gets oxygen into the body (and delivers it to the working muscles). Removes carbon dioxide. Allows an athlete to work for longer (due to increased oxygen supply). Improves cardiovascular endurance.
(1 mark for any of the above)

d)

Label	Anatomical Name	Function
A	Semi-lunar valve	Prevents back flow of blood
B	Septum	Divides left and right sides of the heart / separates oxygenated blood
C	Ventricles	Pump blood out of the heart
D	Atria	Receive blood / push blood through to ventricles

(1 mark for each name, one mark for each function.)

e) i) Increases *(1 mark)*

ii) Increases the delivery of oxygen to the muscles.

f) i) **Cardiac output:** volume of blood ejected from the heart per minute / HR × SV. *(1 mark)*
Effect of exercise on cardiac output: increases. *(1 mark)*

ii) Increases heart rate / increases stroke volume (or any other appropriate description). *(1 mark)*

16 a) i) Increased muscle strength. *(1 mark)*
Improved muscle tone. *(1 mark)*

ii) Repetitions — the number of times you actually move the weights. *(1 mark)*
Sets — the number of times you perform a particular weight activity. This 'activity' may contain a number of repetitions. *(1 mark)*

iii) This is the lowering of fitness levels, due to stopping or decreasing levels of training / This is the reverse effect of progression — the reverse effect is quicker than progression. *(1 mark for just a statement saying what reversibility is, 2 marks if there is some explanation.)*

b) i) **Either**
Sit and reach test — sit with straight legs facing a raised block. Reach forward to push away a slide or marker on the raised block. This is then measured to test the amount of flexibility in the lower back and hamstrings.
or
Use particular stretching exercises (such as bending with straight legs and trying to touch your toes). The distance reached can be measured and compared.
(2 marks for a full description)

ii) Through stretching activities *(1 mark)* such as static stretching, active stretching and passive stretching (or give a specific example). *(1 mark)*
or
Through mobility exercises *(1 mark)* which stretch muscle groups around joints. *(1 mark)*

c) i) Stimulants
Narcotic Analgesics
Diuretics
Peptide Hormones / Mimetics and Analogues / EPO
Beta Blockers
(1 mark each for any two of the above.)

ii) Performers might be tempted to use steroids because they improve performance / allow them train harder and for longer. *(1 mark)*

Effects include:
Increased muscle strength
Allows longer, harder training sessions
Increased competitiveness
Unpleasant side effects
Liver damage and heart disease
Sexual and physique problems
Unpleasant behavioural effects.
(1 mark each for any two suitable effects.)
You can also get marks if you have answered the question in terms of the advantages and disadvantages of taking anabolic steroids.

17 a) i) Television
Radio
Press
Internet
Magazines, books
(1 mark each for three out of the above options.)

ii) Expert analysis in broadcast programmes can highlight good play, moves or action.
Replays of good performances can be used to show good examples of play, style or form.
Promotes awareness of match tactics and techniques used by top level performers.
(1 mark each for any two relevant answers.)

iii) More supporters may be attracted as sports become popularised by the media.
More participants may be attracted to a sport through media coverage raising its profile.
Less people may attend games as they are able to watch on television instead.
Overexposure may lead to a decline in the popularity of some sports.
Media pressure may lead to changes in the rules of some sports to make them more exciting. May also dictate kick-off times to get maximum viewers.
(1 mark each for any two relevant answers.)

b) i) A convention or unwritten rule in an activity *(1 mark)* which usually promotes fair play. Not an enforceable rule, but it's usually observed. *(1 mark)*

ii) E.g.
Soccer — if a player is injured, the opposition kicks the ball out to stop play.
Soccer — after a ball is kicked out to stop play, the ball is given back to the team that kicked it out.
Cricket — batsmen are clapped as they come out to bat.
Shaking hands after a match / thanking officials
(1 mark each for any two relevant examples.)

c) i) A sports person who competes part-time (as well as having another occupation) *(1 mark)*, and who doesn't get paid to take part *(1 mark)*.

ii) A person who competes full-time *(1 mark)* and gets paid for competing — it's their job or career *(1 mark)*.

d) i) Through direct cash payments.
Paying for entry fees.
Providing equipment, apparatus and clothing.
Paying travel costs.
Paying accommodation costs.
(1 mark each for any three of the options above or other sensible answers)

ii) E.g.,
Tobacco firms — because it would be encouraging people to smoke and this is a clearly identified health risk.
Alcohol firms — because it would be encouraging people to drink.
(1 mark for an unacceptable form, 1 mark for explanation.)

18 a) How well a task is completed.

b) i) **Specificity** — Tailoring the training programme to meet the requirements of the activity.
Overload — Fitness can only be improved through training more than you normally do.
Progression — Start slowly and gradually increase the amount that you do.
Meeting individual needs — Tailoring the training programme to suit you, not generalised for a group.
Thresholds of training — levels that you should work within.
Moderation — Be realistic with your training programme — don't attempt too much.
Reversibility — Adaptations will be lost if you stop training.
(1 mark for each principle up to a maximum of three, 1 mark for each matching explanation.)

ii)

Statement from PEP	Principle of Training
A	Specificity
C	Progression
E	Reversibility

c) i) Swelling / pain / lack of movement / bruising / signs of shock. *(1 mark)*

ii) A soft-tissue injury. *(1 mark)*

iii) R.I.C.E. — rest, ice, compression, elevation *(1 mark)*

d) i) A — Patella *(1 mark)*
B — Metatarsals *(1 mark)*
C — Phalanges *(1 mark)*
D — Tarsals *(1 mark)*

ii) Short bones are weight bearing. They also allow mobility around joints. *(1 mark)*

e) i) Fast-twitch muscle fibres. *(1 mark)*

ii) Produce strong, powerful contractions / generate force quickly / allows hurdler to run faster. *(1 mark)*

19 a) It allows them to use their muscles effectively for longer / better stamina. It makes their muscles stronger, improving performance. *(1 mark for either of the above)*

b) Movement is produced by pairs of muscles. *(1 mark)* One muscle contracts while the other relaxes to produce movement in one direction. They swap roles to produce movement in the other direction. *(1 mark)*

c) Parents provide encouragement / equipment / transport.
Schools / PE lessons — coaching, equipment.
Money — children from richer families are likely to have more opportunities.
Local provision of sporting facilities.
Role models
Media — coverage of sport may encourage participation.
(1 mark each for any three of the above.)

d) Facilities like stadiums and swimming pools are often built for major sporting events — local people can use these after the events are over.
Big events raise the profile of sport.
Watching top athletes helps people to learn about sport — tactics, techniques, etc.
Big events promote sporting role models that people seek to emulate.
Big events can make a profit that can be reinvested in sport at a local level.
(1 mark each for any three of the above.)

e) Politics — the government is responsible for providing large scale sporting facilities.
The government can make funding available for top level performers (e.g. through the national lottery).
Political backing is necessary if major sporting events are to be held.
(1 mark each for any two of the above.)
Tradition — a tradition of excellence in a certain sport can encourage more people to play and watch it.
Tradition can make certain sports more socially acceptable, so parents encourage their children to play at a high level.
Tradition can instill a spirit of fair play, for example the 'Olympic spirit'.
(1 mark each for any two of the above.)

f) Intrinsic motivation is a performer's desire to win / perform well or just the enjoyment that comes from taking part. Comes from within *(1 mark)*. Extrinsic motivation is the desire to do well because of the benefits you get from being a winner — trophies, prize money, adulation, sponsorship *(1 mark)*.
Intrinsic motivation is more important because extrinsic motivations may vary between competitions (so performers may not be very motivated when there is less prize money / coverage) *(1 mark)*. Intrinsic motivation is needed when there is no particular external goal — especially during training sessions *(1 mark)*.

g) Top level performers are likely to have been playing for longer / have more experience *(1 mark)*. For example, a top level hockey player might have the experience to anticipate which way a goalkeeper is likely to dive, and therefore have a better chance of scoring *(1 mark)*.
Top level performers are likely to be more consistent because they spend more time practising *(1 mark)*. For example, in archery a novice performer may be able to hit the centre of the target once, but would be unable to do it three times in a row *(1 mark)*.
A high level of coordination may be needed to become a top level performer *(1 mark)*. For example, someone with poor coordination is unlikely to be able to become a professional tennis player *(1 mark)*.
Top level performers are likely to be able to maintain their level of skill under pressure better than novice performers because they usually compete competitively more often *(1 mark)*. For example, a professional golfer is less likely to miss an easy putt when there's a lot of prize money at stake, than a novice *(1 mark)*.
(1 mark for each explanation, one mark for each relevant example, up to a maximum of 8 marks. Other answers are possible.)

Working out your Grade

- Find your average percentage for the whole exam. It's out of 150 marks.
- Look it up in this table to see what grade you got.
  If you're borderline, don't push yourself up a grade — the real examiners won't.

Average %	85+	74 – 84	61 – 73	47 – 60	37 – 46	29 – 36	22 – 28	15 – 21	under 15
Grade	A*	A	B	C	D	E	F	G	U

Important
- Obviously these grades are only a guide — and the more practice you do the better...

Index

Index

Index

CGP

Make sure you're not missing out on another superb CGP revision book that might just save your life...

...order your **free** catalogue today.

CGP customer service is second to none

We work very hard to despatch all orders the **same day** we receive them, and our success rate is currently 99.9%. We send all orders by **overnight courier** or **First Class** post.
If you ring us today you should get your catalogue or book tomorrow. Irresistible, surely?

- Phone: 0870 750 1252   (Mon-Fri, 8.30am to 5.30pm)
- Fax: 0870 750 1292
- e-mail: orders@cgpbooks.co.uk
- Post: CGP, Kirkby in Furness, Cumbria, LA17 7WZ
- Website: www.cgpbooks.co.uk

...or you can ask at any good bookshop.